the *FAMILY* that COOKS TOGETHER

LB

LITTLE, BROWN AND COMPANY

NEW YORK BOSTON LONDON

the *FAMILY that* COOKS TOGETHER

85 Zakarian Family Recipes
from Our Table to Yours

MADELINE & ANNA ZAKARIAN
daughters of **Geoffrey Zakarian**

Little, Brown and Company
Hachette Book Group
1290 Avenue of the Americas
New York, NY 10104
littlebrown.com

First Edition: October 2020

Little, Brown and Company is an imprint of Hachette Book Group, Inc. The Little, Brown name and logo are trademarks of Hachette Book Group, Inc.

The publisher is not responsible for websites (or their content) that are not owned by the publisher.

The Hachette Speakers Bureau provides a wide range of authors for speaking events. To find out more, go to hachettespeakersbureau.com or call (866) 376-6591.

Library of Congress Cataloging-in-Publication Data
Names: Zakarian, Madeline, author. | Zakarian, Anna, author. | Zakarian, Geoffrey, author.
Title: The family that cooks together: 85 Zakarian family recipes from our table to yours / Madeline and Anna Zakarian, daughters of Geoffrey Zakarian.
Description: First edition. | New York : Little, Brown and Company, 2020. | Includes index.
Identifiers: LCCN 2020002129 (print) | LCCN 2020002130 (ebook) | ISBN 978-0-316-53838-1 (paperback) | ISBN 978-0-316-53839-8 (ebook)
Subjects: LCSH: Quick and easy cooking – Juvenile literature. | LCGFT: Cookbooks.
Classification: LCC TX652.5 .Z35 2020 (print) | LCC TX652.5 (ebook) | DDC 641.5/12 – dc23
LC record available at https://lccn.loc.gov/2020002129
LC ebook record available at https://lccn.loc.gov/2020002130

10 9 8 7 6 5 4 3 2 1

Creative direction by Margaret Zakarian

Food styling and recipe testing by Luci Levere

Interior photography by KC and Gail Kratt. Additional photography on pages vi, xii, xvii, 44, 49, 58, 77, 94, 127, 166 (top-center, bottom-right), 167 (top-left, bottom-left) by Amy Doyle: on pages xi, 104, and 167 (bottom-right) by Evan Sung.

Book design by Laura Palese

LSC-C

Printed in the United States of America

THE ZAKARIAN FAMILY, FROM LEFT TO RIGHT:
George, Madeline, Geoffrey, Anna, and Margaret

Madeline,
You crack me up.
—ANNA

Anna,
I love your laugh.
—MADELINE

CONTENTS

Foreword   x
Authors' Note   xiii
Kitchen Tools   xiv
Cheat Sheet   xvi

BREAKFAST   1

Blueberry Crumb Muffins   2
Flourless Banana Muffins   4
Cuckoo Egg and Olive Tartines   5
Amped Avocado Toast   7
Cinnamon Sugar Crullers   8
Greek Sunday Morning   11
Mexican Scrambled Eggs   12
Banana Nutella Sandwiches   15
Middle Eastern Eggs   16
Breakfast Fried Rice   19
Perfect Pancakes   23
Lemon Raspberry Pancakes   24
Fresh Raspberry Sauce   25
On-the-Go Overnight Oats   26

SOUPS, SALADS & SANDWICHES   29

Chop Chop Salad   30
Grapefruit Avocado Salad   31
Country Style Salad   34
Bibb Lettuce with Shallot Vinaigrette   37
Tuna Salad Tartines   38
Cast Iron Grilled Cheese   41
Oven Roasted Tomato Soup   42
Short Stack Turkey Club   45
Parisian Ham Sandwich   46
Chilled Corn Soup   49
Butternut Squash and Apple Soup   50
Grandma's Chicken Noodle Soup   53
Crazy Popcorn Soup   54
Game Day Pork Chili   57

MAIN COURSES   59

Cacio e Pepe   60

Risotto 3X   61

Classic Meatballs with Garlic Bread   64

GZ's Spaghetti Bolognese   66

Linguini with Fresh Clams   67

Steamed Halibut with Coconut Rice   68

Shrimp Scampi   71

Crispy Skin Salmon with Herb Butter   72

Whole Branzino with Braised Fennel   75

Build-Your-Own Fish Tacos   76

Honey Mustard Chicken Skewers   81

Roasted Spatchcock Chicken   82

Crispy Pork Milanese with Arugula Tomato Salad   85

Bistro Hanger Steak with Caramelized Shallots   86

Braised Short Ribs with Egg Noodles   89

The Best Messy Burger   90

SIDES   93

Sautéed Spinach and Garlic   94

Mediterranean Cauliflower   95

Honey Carrots   98

Mustard Potatoes with Apples and Herbs   99

Fragrant Rice Pilaf   101

Steamed Ponzu Broccoli   102

Ratatouille   105

DESSERT   107

Tropical Pineapple and Lime   109

Decadent Brownie Tart   110

Classic French Strawberry Soufflés   113

Heartwarming Apple Crumble   117

Summer Panna Cotta with Peaches   118

Pastel Meringue Clouds   121

Magic Chocolate Mousse   122

Vanilla Bean Shortbread   125

Whipped Cream Forever   126

SNACKS   129

Olive Oil Granola Bars   130

Power-Up Snack Balls   133

Creamy Hummus with Crudités   134

Everything Cheddar Crackers   136

Homemade Potato Chips   137

Sea Salt Kale Chips   141

Soft Baked Pretzels and Purple Mustard   142

Tomato and Herb Focaccia   145

DRINKS   147

Hibiscus Iced Tea   148

Cucumber Cooler   151

Grapefruit Raspberry Sparkler   152

Rosemary Blush   154

Simple Syrup   155

Strawberry Banana Smoothie Plus   156

Dreamy Cookies and Cream Milkshake   159

Beetroot Latte   162

Premier Hot Chocolate   165

Note of Thanks   *168*

Index   *169*

FOREWORD

The Family That Cooks Together came about after the first time I met Iron Chef Geoffrey Zakarian.

When I learned that cooking was a family affair for him and his daughters, Anna and Madeline, I just couldn't get the idea of a Zakarian family cookbook out of my head. Over the course of publishing this book, I've had the pleasure of getting to know the Zakarian family and discovering all the incredible ways food brings them together. It was inspiring to see parents and children cooking alongside one another, and to learn that the Zakarians' tradition dates back generations.

Cooking was a big part of my life growing up as well. Back then, everything was very hands-on and traditional. I still remember my mother sending me to get the fruit she kept in the root cellar after stone fruit season. It's such a funny thing to kids nowadays, the idea of a root cellar, but that's how we did things. My sisters and I spent hours in the kitchen with our mother, making recipes that had been passed down through the generations. The house was always filled with delicious smells. I look back fondly on those memories—there's nothing like home cooking, and there's *especially* nothing like home cooking when you help make it yourself.

I know that *The Family That Cooks Together* will create many happy memories for countless families. From Game Day Pork Chili to Cast Iron Grilled Cheese to Breakfast Fried Rice, the absolutely delicious recipes in this book are destined to become family favorites that you return to again and again. After all, nothing brings a family together like a meal everyone loves—and who would know better than a foodie family like the Zakarians? I'm thrilled that I could help such a wonderfully talented family bring these tried and tested recipes from their table to yours.

Bon appétit!

—James Patterson

Ratatouille
PAGE 105

AUTHORS' NOTE

As the daughters of a professional chef, our lives have involved food in so many special ways.

From the moment we each came home from the hospital, we've been hearing a symphony of kitchen sounds in the background of our every day—pots clanking, ice crunching, blender whirring, liquids boiling, shells cracking, and the constant whoosh of the refrigerator door. This playlist has been the soundtrack of our lives, building up our love for food. We've spent countless hours watching our parents prepare meals at home and run exciting restaurants at work, which has allowed us to sample so many different dishes. With all the listening, watching, and tasting, we unknowingly received a different kind of education.

Even in our youth, we've realized that food is so much more than it seems. As avid eaters, amateur cooks, and lovers of hospitality, we've seen firsthand the joy that gathering around a table brings. Along our way, we've collected special memories from delicious meals and are excited to share them with you.

This book is for home cooks of all ages, and we wrote it with an important piece of advice in mind: Cook for others, not yourself. The chance to be a great chef isn't about you, but rather other people. You can train yourself to be skilled in the kitchen, but your cooking will taste much better with friends or family there to enjoy it. Remembering this in your culinary adventures can keep you happy and humble, and will encourage you to continue. We have learned that spending time together through food has kept our family close, and we think you will find the same.

We wish you many days of happy cooking ahead, and remember to have fun making noise in the kitchen!

—Madeline & Anna

KITCHEN TOOLS

Here's a secret, just between us: You don't need
any fancy kitchen tools to cook delicious meals. You could
make almost anything with the following: a sheet pan, a
large sauté pan, a saucepan, a 9-inch chef knife, a paring
knife, a wooden spoon, a whisk, a spatula, and a good-sized
cutting board. You probably have all this already!

But there are a few fun bells and whistles
that can make you feel like a pro in the kitchen.
Here are our absolute favorites:

FINE-MESH STRAINER A pro tool for sure, a
fine-mesh strainer is much more useful than a
regular strainer. The closely knit metal catches
all the tiny bits of food in its basket and allows
only pure liquid to pass. Your finished dish will
have a smooth taste without any unpleasant bits.
If you don't have one, no worries! You can use
cheesecloth to strain instead.

FISH SPATULA This is one of our favorite tools,
though we surprisingly rarely use it for fish. The
extended and oblong shape of the spatula gives
you more control when you need to lift or flip a
variety of items.

FOOD PROCESSOR The time that a food
processor saves is worth the investment in one.
Essentially, it is a bowl fitted with a sharp blade
powered by a motor. The blade chops or minces
foods without pushing too much air inside the
food, the way a blender would, so you cannot
always substitute a blender for a food processor.
We recommend buying a simple sturdy one
powered by a strong motor and steering clear

of the models with too many extras as it can get
quickly overcomplicated.

FORCEPS The most "cheffy" thing on the list!
Kitchen forceps are giant metal tweezers used
to place garnishes and pieces of food in just
the right spot. You can also use them to move
delicate things when cooking. So fun to use!

HAND JUICER If you only need a small amount
of juice, using this clamp-like tool is much easier
and quicker than an electric juicer. Helpful
tip: Never buy pre-packaged citrus juice. It's
healthier to freshly squeeze a lemon or lime
yourself.

IMMERSION BLENDER This is a handheld stick
that you put into a container or pot to blend the
ingredients. It's safer than transferring hot liquid
to a blender, like in soup recipes. Some models
even come with a potato masher or a whisk
attachment, so you can whip or process in the
same bowl you started with. Less dishes to wash
are always a plus!

INTERNET   We consider this essential, because when we don't understand something in a recipe, we can easily go online to figure it out by searching images or watching recipe preparation videos. Also, if we cannot find an ingredient in the store, we simply order it online.

MANDOLINE   This thin slicer gives you speed and consistency in your cuts, which are two cornerstones of traditional French cooking. However, it can be very dangerous, so make sure to get a safe-slice version to protect your fingers.

MEAT THERMOMETER   Our dad says this is the most important thing to have when cooking meat. With this tool, you won't have to guess how "done" a piece of meat is.

MICROPLANE ZESTERS/GRATERS   This brand works extremely well, and their zesting/grating tools can be used to finely grate citrus skins, nutmeg, cinnamon sticks...the list goes on and on. Just be careful not to scrape your hand or finger on the sharp part.

MUDDLER   Handy for crushing and mashing small foods, we use muddlers to do everything from smashing avocado to crunching up whole almonds. For making drinks, it helps to release the oil in herbs like mint.

OFFSET SPATULA (SMALL)   This tool makes frosting super easy, but we also grab it when we need a small tool to spread or lift food.

OVEN THERMOMETER   Making sure your oven is the right temperature is a pro move. You might be surprised at the difference between the temperature you set your oven to and what the thermometer tells you when you manually place it inside.

PASTRY BRUSH   Having a food-specific brush lets you coat things in oils or melted butter with more precision than drizzling—and with less mess than using your hands.

PIPING BAG   Pastry bags are a fun item to have for piping whipped cream or decorating a cake. Some bags come with fancy tips for super-decorative garnishes and toppings. If you're in a pinch, you can use a zip-top bag instead of a piping bag: Fill the bag, cut off a bottom corner, and you're ready to squeeze.

RAMEKINS   These cute, multipurpose containers are one of our essential picks for cooking and serving. They're great for baking individual portions or for serving snacks and dips.

SPIDER   In cooking, a spider is a long, spoon-like tool, with a metal strainer on one end and a flat wooden stick for the handle. It allows you to strain and move pasta or small vegetables, like peas, out of boiling water without having to carry a large, scalding pot to the sink. It's also useful when you need to carefully place ingredients into already boiling water. Safety first!

SPURTLE   Fun to say and handy to use, this Scottish tool is a hybrid of a spoon and a spatula. The curved shape gives you the holding power of a spoon, but with the length and flatness similar to a spatula. It can reach all corners of your pot in one easy swoosh.

CHEAT SHEET

Here are some tips that will make your
food more delicious, guaranteed. Trust us, we
learned them from an Iron Chef!

1 When shopping for ingredients, read the labels. Manufacturers often sneak in weird things you wouldn't expect.

2 Place one damp paper towel under your cutting board to keep the board from slipping or moving around.

3 Use sea salt or kosher salt for cooking. We like the brand Baleine. Their salt labeled "fine" for general seasoning and cooking is our go-to. Save the large flake salt for finishing only.

4 You don't have to spend a lot of money to make good food, but there are a few ingredients where higher quality makes a difference. Splurge on high-end vanilla extract, vinegars, and dark chocolate.

5 Buy spices in small quantities and replace them in your pantry every year. As spices age, the oils evaporate, making them less flavorful. The fresher, the better!

6 Make sure your pan heats to the right temperature before adding ingredients.

7 When boiling water to cook pasta, add salt to the water so it's as salty as the sea. This raises the boiling point, which helps the noodles cook faster and flavors the pasta as it absorbs the salted water when cooking.

8 Always salt and pepper raw beef, pork, poultry, and fish on all sides before cooking.

9 Before cutting beef, pork, and poultry after it's cooked, let it rest for at least 10 minutes. To keep the meat warm in the meantime, you can make a loose tinfoil tent over it.

10 Be sure to taste food as you go and season accordingly. You don't want to serve something without having tasted it, so remember to adjust the seasoning along the way.

11 When baking, use room-temperature eggs. Useful tip: Place the eggs in a bowl of warm water to speed up the warming process.

12 The freezer is your friend! When you have spare time, cook or bake your favorite meals and snacks, then freeze until you're ready to use.

13 Don't stress out over not having the right tools or electrics. You can always improvise when in the kitchen to find something that works, including mixing, whisking, or chopping by hand.

BREAKFAST

BLUEBERRY CRUMB MUFFINS

Everyone wants that one blueberry muffin with loads of crumble on top, so we decided to share a recipe that would guarantee crumbs for all! We amped up the traditional take even more by including lemon zest in the batter, giving the muffin some brightness. *Makes 12 muffins*

FOR THE CRUMB TOPPING

6 tablespoons (¾ stick) unsalted butter, melted

1½ cups all-purpose flour

½ cup granulated sugar

¼ teaspoon kosher salt

FOR THE MUFFINS

3 cups all-purpose flour

1 cup granulated sugar

1 tablespoon baking powder

½ teaspoon kosher salt

12 tablespoons (1½ sticks) unsalted butter, melted and cooled

1 cup sour cream

¼ cup whole milk

2 large eggs

1 teaspoon vanilla extract

Grated zest of 1 lemon

2 cups fresh blueberries, plus additional for topping

HELPFUL TOOLS

Microplane zester

12-cup muffin pan

Cupcake liners or nonstick cooking spray

1 Preheat the oven to 325°F. Lightly spray the cups of a standard 12-cup muffin pan with cooking spray or line with cupcake liners.

2 To make the crumb topping: In a small mixing bowl with a fork, toss together the melted butter, flour, sugar, and salt until crumbly. Set aside.

3 To make the muffins: In large bowl, whisk together the flour, sugar, baking powder, and salt. In a separate bowl, whisk together the melted butter, sour cream, milk, eggs, vanilla extract, and lemon zest.

4 Add the wet ingredients to the dry, then carefully fold with a spatula until the flour mixture is almost incorporated. Add the blueberries and fold until the fruit is evenly distributed and a few streaks of flour remain. It is important not to overwork the batter; a few lumps are okay.

5 Divide the batter evenly among the 12 muffin cups. Top each muffin with an additional 5 or 6 blueberries and then sprinkle with the crumb topping. Bake for 25 to 30 minutes, until a toothpick inserted in the center of a muffin comes out clean. Serve once the muffins are cool enough to handle, or pack them for an on-the-go breakfast.

In the summer, buy as many wild blueberries as you can and freeze them in sandwich bags to use later. Wild summer blueberries have a smaller size that are well-suited for muffins. Plus, they have a delicious taste that's a nice treat during the winter months.

**Flourless
Banana Muffins**
PAGE 4

**Blueberry
Crumb Muffins**
PAGE 2

FLOURLESS BANANA MUFFINS

These muffins are so irresistible that they're sure to be snatched up as soon as the pan lands on the counter. They most definitely exist in "sweet treat" land, but no worries, because they're guilt-free with no flour or granulated sugar. Choose a dark chocolate chip with zero milk, and each bite will be both dairy-free and gluten-free. **Makes 12 muffins**

1 teaspoon baking soda

1 teaspoon baking powder

1 teaspoon ground cinnamon

½ teaspoon kosher salt

2 very ripe large bananas, mashed

2 large eggs, lightly whisked

¼ cup honey

1 teaspoon vanilla extract

1 cup natural organic almond butter

½ cup mini dark chocolate chips

Sliced almonds, for topping, optional

HELPFUL TOOLS

12-cup muffin pan

Cupcake liners or nonstick cooking spray

1 Preheat the oven to 350°F. Liberally spray the cups of a standard 12-cup muffin pan with cooking spray or line with cupcake liners.

2 In a small bowl, gently whisk the baking soda, baking powder, cinnamon, and salt. In a medium bowl, whisk together the bananas and eggs, then in the following order add the honey, vanilla extract, and almond butter. Add the dry ingredients to the wet, and fold in the chocolate chips.

3 Distribute the batter equally (about ¼ cup per muffin) among the muffin cups and top each with almond slices, if you like. Bake for 15 minutes and test for doneness. The muffins should spring back when lightly pressed. If not done, bake a few minutes longer, but watch closely, as they can quickly dry out. Once out of the oven, remove each muffin from the pan and let cool before storing or eating.

If you do not have ripe bananas, you can place the bananas on a sheet pan and bake in a 300°F oven for about 15 minutes. Let them cool before using.

Recipe pictured on page 3

CUCKOO EGG & OLIVE TARTINES

If your family is all on different wake-up schedules and can't sit down together for breakfast, these tartines do the trick. They can sit without "dying," like other egg dishes might, making them a great choice if you're hosting brunch. The savory tapenade brings a refreshing contrast to hardboiled eggs, and pairs perfectly with the crunch of an English muffin and arugula. Feel free to use store-bought tapenade to save time. Cuckoo! *Serves 4*

FOR THE EGGS

4 large eggs

FOR THE TAPENADE

½ cup brine-cured black olives, such as kalamata, pitted

2 tablespoons capers, drained

2 tablespoons chopped fresh Italian parsley

1 small garlic clove, chopped

1 anchovy fillet, chopped

2 tablespoons extra virgin olive oil

TO ASSEMBLE AND FINISH

4 English muffins, split and toasted

1 cup baby arugula

1 tablespoon extra virgin olive oil

Kosher salt, for sprinkling

1 lemon, cut into wedges

HELPFUL TOOLS

Mini food processor (or chop by hand)

Hard-boiled egg slicer, optional

1 To make the hard-boiled eggs: Fill a medium pot halfway with water and bring to a boil over high heat. Carefully lower the eggs into the pot and cook for 12 minutes. Remove the eggs from the water and allow to cool for about 10 minutes, then crack and peel under cold running water. Rinse and remove any remaining bits of shell.

2 To make the tapenade: In a mini food processor, combine the olives, capers, parsley, garlic, and anchovy. Pulse to make a chunky paste. With the machine running, drizzle in the olive oil to make an almost smooth paste. (You may chop and mix by hand if a mini is not available.) Scrape the tapenade into a bowl and set aside.

3 To assemble and finish: Place the toasted English muffins on four plates. Spread each half with about 1 tablespoon tapenade. In a small bowl, toss the arugula with the olive oil, then divide among the tartines. Cut each hard-boiled egg into six slices using a slicer or by hand. Lay three slices of egg on each English muffin half. Sprinkle the tartines with salt and serve with a lemon wedge. Refrigerate any remaining tapenade for next time.

Recipe pictured on page 6

Amped
Avocado Toast
PAGE 7

Cuckoo Egg &
Olive Tartines
PAGE 5

AMPED AVOCADO TOAST

New Yorkers have gone mad for avocado toast, us included! Topping it with a fried egg and prosciutto makes a great breakfast before we head to school. We suggest using sourdough, but feel free to choose any bread, as long as the slices are not too thin. *Serves 4*

1 loaf sourdough bread

2 avocados, ripe but not soft

1 teaspoon Chardonnay vinegar or white wine vinegar

Kosher salt and freshly ground black pepper

8 slices prosciutto di Parma

1 tablespoon extra virgin olive oil

4 large eggs, cracked into 4 small individual cups

HELPFUL TOOLS

Serrated knife

1   With a serrated knife, slice four ½-inch-thick slices of bread. (Freeze any remaining bread for another use.) Toast in the toaster until golden brown.

2   Cut the avocados in half and carefully remove the pits. Scoop out the flesh into a small bowl and mash lightly with a fork, leaving some small chunks. Add the vinegar and 2 pinches of salt and stir until combined. Divide the avocado mash among the four toast slices and spread to the edges. Lay two pieces of prosciutto on top of the avocado mash. Set aside.

3   In a large sauté pan, heat the olive oil over medium heat. Add the eggs, being careful not to break the yolks. Fry until the whites are set, about 5 minutes. You want the yolks to remain runny. Remove from the heat.

4   Top each avocado and prosciutto toast with a fried egg. Season with salt and pepper.

If you prefer, you can crisp up the prosciutto by laying the pieces on a parchment-lined sheet pan and baking in a 300°F oven for 15 to 20 minutes, depending on thickness.

CINNAMON SUGAR CRULLERS

These dreamy fried bundles of doughnutty perfection deliver in a huge way. Nothing compares to that crispy on the outside and chewy sweetness on the inside taste of a just-baked cruller. It's worth the time it takes to master this recipe! *Makes 10 to 12 crullers*

FOR THE CINNAMON SUGAR

1 cup granulated sugar

1 tablespoon ground cinnamon

FOR THE CRULLERS

½ cup whole milk

½ cup water

8 tablespoons (1 stick) unsalted butter

1 tablespoon granulated sugar

1½ teaspoons kosher salt

1¼ cups all-purpose flour

3 large eggs

1 large egg white, lightly beaten

Grated zest of 1 lemon

2 quarts canola oil

HELPFUL TOOLS

Microplane zester

Stand mixer with paddle attachment

Silicone spatula

Large Dutch oven and candy thermometer, or a deep fryer

Parchment paper

Sheet pan

Nonstick cooking spray

Metal tongs

Piping bag with large star tip

1 To make the cinnamon sugar: In a medium mixing bowl, whisk the sugar and cinnamon until combined. Set aside.

2 To make the crullers: In a large saucepan, bring the milk, water, butter, sugar, and salt just to a boil over medium-high heat. Add the flour and quickly stir with a spoon. Continue to cook, stirring constantly, for about 3 minutes, until the mixture starts to pull away from the sides of the pan.

3 Transfer to the bowl of a stand mixer fitted with a paddle attachment. Starting on speed one, beat the flour mixture for a few minutes until cooled slightly. Scrape down the sides of the bowl with the spatula. Continue mixing and add the eggs, one at a time, allowing them to fully mix before adding the next. Add the egg white and lemon zest, mix to incorporate, then remove the bowl from the mixer. Scrape the batter from the paddle with the spatula and scrape down the sides of the bowl again. Let the batter sit while heating the oil.

4 In a large Dutch oven over medium-high to high heat or a tabletop deep fryer, heat the oil to 360°F. Cut a piece of parchment paper into ten to twelve 3x3-inch rectangles. Lay the squares on a sheet pan and spray lightly with nonstick cooking spray. Fit a star tip into the piping bag so it peeks out of the end and fill the bag with the dough. Pipe a uniform circle onto each square to make a doughnut shape, overlapping batter as you finish each circle.

5 Once the oil has reached 360°F, in batches, carefully place the crullers in the oil, top side down. Remove the parchment square with tongs. Fry on the first side for about 5 minutes, or until the batter starts to erupt on the top. Flip over with tongs and fry on second side for an additional 5 minutes, or until golden brown. Remove from the oil and drain on a paper towel–lined plate. Toss the hot crullers immediately in the cinnamon sugar and serve.

GREEK SUNDAY MORNING

We are completely bored of the usual yogurt parfaits, piled with layers of yogurt, berries, and granola. There's too much digging to reach those yummy berries. Our version is inspired by a restaurant our parents opened in California, and just like the state, this yogurt dish is sunny, has fresh, delicious ingredients, and gives you lots of room in the bowl. So long, tall parfait glasses! Hello, Greek Sunday Morning! *Serves 4*

1 quart Greek yogurt, drained in the fridge overnight in a cheesecloth-lined fine-mesh strainer placed over a bowl

1 ripe avocado, pitted, peeled, and cut into medium chunks

1 pink grapefruit, peeled and segmented into supremes (see box)

2 small oranges, peeled and segmented into supremes (see box)

1 cup raspberries

1 cup granola, optional

2 tablespoons honey

12 small fresh mint sprigs

HELPFUL TOOLS

Cheesecloth

Offset spatula

1   Divide the drained yogurt among four roomy breakfast bowls, placing it in the center, away from the sides of the bowls. With a spoon or offset spatula, spread the yogurt in an even layer.

2   Lay the avocado chunks on top of the yogurt randomly.

3   Scatter pieces of pink grapefruit and orange segments around the yogurt. Then drop raspberries onto the remaining open area of the yogurt. Sprinkle with granola, if you like.

4   Drizzle with honey and garnish with mint sprigs.

How to Segment Citrus Fruit into Supremes

With a serrated knife, cut the end off the grapefruit or other citrus so it can sit flat on a cutting board. Slice off the peel and pith in a curving downward motion, following the natural edge of the fruit and leaving just the flesh and membranes. Then, hold the peeled grapefruit in your hand and very carefully cut alongside each membrane to cut out each fruit segment, dropping them into a small bowl. This gives you just the pure fruit with none of the pith or membrane. Squeeze any juice from the membrane piece into a large bowl and save for later use. (Don't hesitate to watch a video of this technique online.)

MEXICAN SCRAMBLED EGGS

Choosing this for breakfast feels forbidden—when you add shredded cheese and tortilla chips, it is like a "no one is watching" nacho antic—but this recipe makes the cut. It's the perfect easy addition to a weekly a.m. meal routine. Chips at breakfast—yes, please! *Serves 4*

3 tablespoons extra virgin olive oil

4 corn tortillas, cut into 8 wedges each

Kosher salt

6 large eggs

1 to 2 tablespoons unsalted butter

2 scallions (both the green and white parts), trimmed and sliced

1 cup shredded Mexican cheese blend

HELPFUL TOOLS

Silicone spatula

1   Heat the olive oil in a large skillet over medium-high heat. Add the tortilla wedges and fry until crispy, 6 to 8 minutes. Remove from the pan and season immediately with salt. Set aside.

2   In a medium bowl, whisk the eggs with 1 teaspoon salt until smooth. Wipe out the pan carefully and return to medium heat. Melt the butter, then add the scallions and sauté for 2 minutes. Add the eggs and cook, using a silicone spatula to stir constantly, making wide circles. The eggs should thicken quickly. Once the eggs are almost set and large, soft curds have formed, remove from the heat and gently fold in the cheese.

3   Divide the eggs among four plates and top with crumbled tortilla chips.

 If preferred, use store-bought corn tortilla chips and skip Step 1.

BANANA NUTELLA SANDWICHES

This qualifies as the biggest breakfast crowd-pleaser we know! It has the same inviting temptation as grilled cheese (crunchy bread and a warm, gooey inside) and can parade as dessert (sweet hazelnutty deliciousness), yet genuinely passes the test for an a.m. meal, all thanks to potassium-rich bananas and a healthy dose of protein from nuts. If you want to make this for a group, keep the finished sandwiches warm by placing them in a 200°F oven on a sheet pan with a rack while you build the others. *Serves 4*

1 cup Nutella

8 slices white or wheat bread

½ cup almond butter

2 ripe bananas, peeled and sliced into ½-inch-thick rounds

½ cup hazelnuts, toasted and roughly chopped

6 tablespoons (¾ stick) salted butter, at room temperature

1   For each sandwich, spread 2 tablespoons Nutella on one slice of bread. On a second slice of bread, spread 1 tablespoon almond butter. Top each Nutella side with banana slices in a single layer, using half a banana for each sandwich. Sprinkle 2 tablespoons hazelnuts on the side of slices with the almond butter, pressing in lightly with the back of a spoon. Join both pieces of bread together to make a sandwich.

2   Melt 3 tablespoons butter in a large sauté pan over medium heat. Add the sandwiches and cook on the first side until golden brown, about 5 minutes.

3   Add the remaining 3 tablespoons butter to the pan and allow to melt. Flip over the sandwiches, moving them around the pan to distribute the butter. Cook on the second side until golden brown, 3 to 5 minutes. Remove from the heat and place the sandwiches on a cutting board. Cool for a few minutes before cutting in half to serve.

 A panini press could be used instead of a sauté pan.

MIDDLE EASTERN EGGS

During the holidays, our grandmother Marie cooks traditional Middle Eastern dishes for our large extended Lebanese family, much to everyone's delight. There are always leftover pieces of raw lamb she doesn't need, so over the years, she started frying them with pine nuts and onions that she'd then scramble together with eggs for breakfast the next morning. As soon as the dish hits the table, we jump to get it on our plates. Because we enjoy this meal so much, we now shop for lamb at all times of year just to make the breakfast "leftover dish" for ourselves! The picture shows traditional Syrian bread which can be hard to find, but regular pita works just as well to scoop up those delicious eggs.

Serves 4 to 6

2 tablespoons extra virgin olive oil

1 medium yellow onion, diced

¾ pound ground lamb

¾ teaspoon ground cinnamon

1¼ teaspoons kosher salt, plus more for seasoning

¼ teaspoon freshly ground black pepper

¼ cup pine nuts, toasted

6 large eggs

2 tablespoons unsalted butter

¼ cup coarsely chopped Italian parsley

Warm pita bread, for serving

HELPFUL TOOLS

Cast iron skillet

Silicone spatula or wooden spoon

1 Heat the olive oil in a large skillet (preferably cast iron) over medium heat. Add the onion and cook until softened, about 5 minutes. Add the lamb, cinnamon, salt, and pepper. Cook, stirring occasionally, until the lamb is browned and cooked through, about 10 minutes. Add the pine nuts.

2 Meanwhile, in a small mixing bowl, whisk the eggs and season with salt and pepper. When lamb is fully cooked, push the mixture to the edge of the pan. Add the butter to the center of the pan and allow to melt. Pour in the eggs. Using a silicone spatula or wooden spoon, stir the eggs in large circles, allowing large curds to form. Once the eggs are almost cooked, incorporate the lamb mixture into the eggs and remove from the heat.

3 Divide the eggs among plates, garnish with parsley, and serve with warm pita bread.

BREAKFAST FRIED RICE

When you have the chance to order in an Asian meal, always save the extra containers of steamed rice. Our dad taught us that the best way to make fried rice is with day-old steamed rice. Shocking, we know, but it's true! He regularly fixes this for breakfast, and even Mom approves, as it has eggs and a bunch of whatever leftovers are in the fridge. Plus, it keeps us filled straight through to lunch. Once you learn the basic method of frying the rice, experiment by adding your own choice of vegetables. *Serves 4*

2 tablespoons sesame oil, divided

1 carrot, peeled and shredded

1 small yellow onion, diced

1 teaspoon peeled, grated fresh ginger

1 cup leftover cooked vegetables, such as broccoli and peas, chopped

4 cups day-old steamed brown or white rice, at room temperature

⅓ cup reduced-sodium soy sauce

¼ cup teriyaki sauce

2 tablespoons rice wine vinegar

3 large eggs, whisked in small bowl

3 scallions (green and white parts), thinly sliced

1 tablespoon sesame seeds, toasted

¼ cup chopped fresh cilantro

HELPFUL TOOLS

Silicone spatula or wooden spoon

1   In a large skillet over medium heat, heat 1 tablespoon of the sesame oil. Once shimmering, add the carrot, onion, and ginger and cook until softened, about 5 minutes.

2   Add the vegetables and rice, breaking up any rice clumps with a silicone spatula or wooden spoon. Continue to cook until the vegetables and rice are heated through, about 5 minutes. Add the soy sauce, teriyaki sauce, and vinegar and stir.

3   Push the rice mixture to the edges of the pan and add the remaining 1 tablespoon sesame oil to the center. Add the eggs all at once and cook, stirring constantly, until large curds form and the eggs are cooked through. Incorporate the rice and vegetable mixture into the eggs, stirring to combine. Remove from the heat.

4   Garnish with the scallions, toasted sesame seeds, and cilantro. Divide among bowls and serve.

Perfect Pancakes
PAGE 23

Lemon Raspberry Pancakes
PAGE 24

PERFECT PANCAKES

You'll never regret having a perfect pancake recipe in your back pocket. There are many recipes out there, but this one will give you fluffy cakes that are not too dense and are great-tasting, even without lots of toppings. Of course, you can add many things to jazz up the pancakes, but a simple, well-made batter that's fried correctly and drizzled with maple syrup ties together what we have learned about cooking: Find the best ingredients, treat them simply and properly, and you will end up with something delicious. Very important note: Check the ingredients of your "maple" syrup, and if it's made from corn syrup and food coloring, please discard! Seek out 100 percent pure maple syrup. It'll make your pancakes so much better. *Serves 4*

2 cups all-purpose flour

2 teaspoons baking powder

1 teaspoon baking soda

1 teaspoon kosher salt

2 large eggs, whisked

2 cups buttermilk or goat milk kefir

2 tablespoons 100 percent pure maple syrup, plus more for serving

2 tablespoons unsalted butter, melted, plus more butter for serving

½ teaspoon vanilla extract

2 tablespoons avocado oil or other neutral oil

HELPFUL TOOLS

Fine-mesh strainer

1 Sift the flour, baking powder, baking soda, and salt together in a medium bowl. In another medium bowl, whisk the eggs, buttermilk, maple syrup, melted butter, and vanilla. Add the wet ingredients to the dry and whisk until almost smooth. Strain the pancake batter through a fine-mesh strainer.

2 Heat a large nonstick skillet over medium heat. Add the oil and tilt pan to spread the oil around. Using a ¼-cup measure, drop about 4 portions of batter into the pan. Cook until bubbles start to form, about 3 minutes. Flip the pancakes and cook for 2 to 3 minutes more, or until golden brown.

3 Remove the pancakes from the pan and serve immediately with butter and maple syrup.

LEMON RASPBERRY PANCAKES

At grand hotels, the breakfast menu always offers a dressed-up version of pancakes, taking them beyond the usual blueberries or chocolate chips. When we make our own fancy combination of lemon and raspberry at home, we daydream about breakfast in bed, room service, and being on vacation. And in this recipe, there's a secret cooking trick to get the edges nice and crispy. *Serves 4*

2 cups all-purpose flour

2 teaspoons baking powder

1 teaspoon baking soda

1 teaspoon kosher salt

2 large eggs, whisked

2 cups buttermilk or goat milk kefir

2 tablespoons 100 percent pure maple syrup, plus more for serving

2 tablespoons unsalted butter, melted, plus more butter for serving

½ teaspoon vanilla extract

Grated zest of 1 lemon

2 tablespoons avocado oil or other neutral oil, plus more for squeeze bottle

1 pint raspberries, washed

Fresh Raspberry Sauce (page 25), optional

HELPFUL TOOLS

Microplane zester

Fine-mesh strainer

Small squeeze bottle

1   Sift the flour, baking powder, baking soda, and salt together in a medium bowl. In another medium bowl, whisk the eggs, buttermilk, maple syrup, melted butter, and vanilla. Add the wet ingredients to the dry and whisk until almost smooth. Strain the pancake batter through a fine-mesh strainer. Gently fold in the lemon zest.

2   Heat a large nonstick skillet over medium heat. Add the 2 tablespoons oil and tilt the pan to spread it around. Using a ¼-cup measure, drop batter into pan. Using a small squeeze bottle of avocado or other neutral oil, drizzle a bit of the oil just on the outside edge around each pancake. Dot the surface of each pancake with several raspberries. Cook the pancakes until bubbles start to form and they look opaque, 3 to 5 minutes. Flip the pancakes and cook for 3 to 5 minutes more.

3   Remove the pancakes from the pan and serve immediately with maple syrup, raspberry sauce, if you like, and the remaining fresh raspberries.

Recipe pictured on page 22

Fresh Raspberry Sauce

MAKES 1 CUP

1 pint fresh raspberries

1 tablespoon granulated sugar

1 tablespoon water

1 teaspoon lemon juice

Combine the raspberries, sugar, water, and lemon juice
a saucepan. Cook over medium heat, stirring, until the
raspberries break down, the sugar dissolves, and the sauce
is heated through, 5 to 7 minutes. Remove from the heat.
Cool to room temperature to allow the mixture to thicken.
Store in an airtight container for up to 5 days.

TIP *If you prefer a smoother texture, press the
cooled sauce through a fine-mesh strainer to
remove seeds and any remaining pieces of fruit.*

ON-THE-GO OVERNIGHT OATS

When you need to zip out the door in the morning, plan ahead the night before with this simple recipe. Instead of using a large container, use individual glass jars so your breakfast is ready to grab and go in the a.m. No fuss or mess! This recipe is one of our favorites during the summer when we sail and do outside sports. *Serves 2 to 3, depending on serving container size*

1 cup rolled oats

2 cups almond milk

¼ cup chia seeds

2 tablespoons 100 percent pure maple syrup

2 tablespoons cashew butter

½ teaspoon ground cinnamon

½ teaspoon kosher salt

Toppings: your choice of diced mango, berries, toasted chopped nuts, seeds, toasted coconut, and granola

HELPFUL TOOLS
6- to 8-ounce glass jars

1 Whisk together the oats, milk, chia seeds, maple syrup, cashew butter, cinnamon, and salt in a medium bowl. Divide between two 8-ounce jars and screw on the lids. Shake to combine and refrigerate overnight.

2 The following morning, unscrew the lid, add toppings of choice, and enjoy!

SOUPS, SALADS & SANDWICHES

CHOP CHOP SALAD

This salad is perfect at home alongside a casual pasta, or even prepared for a lunch out of the house. Salad is often an overlooked item for a lunch box, since it usually gets soggy. But with this recipe, the hearty vitamin-packed veggies start off crunchy and stay perfectly crisp until you're ready to eat.

Serves 4 to 6

FOR THE DRESSING

½ cup extra virgin olive oil

¼ cup red wine vinegar

1 teaspoon dried oregano

½ teaspoon kosher salt

¼ teaspoon freshly ground black pepper

FOR THE SALAD

1 cup chopped romaine hearts, inside white leaves only (discard or reserve outside leaves), washed and cut into bite-size pieces

1 large carrot, peeled and cut into bite-size pieces

1 stalk celery, cut into bite-size pieces

¼ cup celery leaves, light green leaves only

½ red bell pepper, cut into bite-size pieces

1 cup chickpeas, rinsed

½ cup coarsely grated Parmesan cheese

1   To make the dressing: In a small bowl, whisk together the olive oil, vinegar, and oregano. Season with salt and pepper and whisk until emulsified.

2   To assemble the salad: In a large salad bowl, combine the romaine, carrot, celery, celery leaves, bell pepper, chickpeas, and Parmesan and toss with two large spoons.

3   Drizzle the salad with a light coating of dressing and toss again. You may not need all the dressing. Extra dressing can be stored in the refrigerator for up to 1 week.

Make and store the dressing in a small portable jar, which is easy to shake and then use to dress the salad once it's time to eat.

Recipe pictured on page 32

GRAPEFRUIT AVOCADO SALAD

The bright acidic nature of grapefruit pairs extremely well with the smooth taste of avocado. We often make this as a side salad when we're having a fun taco night. Here's a tip: Be sure to slice the onion thin enough so it doesn't overpower the other flavors yet is still thick enough to give you a bit of crunch. *Serves 4 to 6*

¼ small red onion, thinly sliced

2 large pink grapefruit, peeled and segmented into supremes (see box, page 11), juice reserved

2 tablespoons red wine vinegar

1 teaspoon honey

Kosher salt and freshly ground black pepper

6 tablespoons extra virgin olive oil

2 ripe avocados, pitted, peeled, and cubed

2 bunches watercress, tough stems trimmed, then washed and dried

HELPFUL TOOLS

Serrated knife

1 Fill a small bowl with ice water and add the onion. While you prepare the salad, let the onion soak, which removes some of the bite and crisps it up.

2 In a large bowl, combine the grapefruit juice, vinegar, and honey, whisk to combine, and season with salt and pepper. Whisk in the olive oil in a slow, steady stream to make a smooth dressing. Add the grapefruit segments, avocados, and watercress.

3 Drain the onion and pat dry. Add to the salad and toss gently to coat with dressing. Adjust the seasoning and serve.

Recipe pictured on page 33

Country Style Salad
PAGE 34

Chop Chop Salad
PAGE 30

**Grapefruit
Avocado Salad**
PAGE 31

COUNTRY STYLE SALAD

This salad is awesome for family meals, plus it looks pretty either tossed or set out on a big platter for sharing. You can even make it count as a complete meal by adding some grilled chicken or shrimp. *Serves 4 to 6*

½ cup extra virgin olive oil

3 tablespoons red wine vinegar

1 teaspoon minced garlic

½ teaspoon dried oregano, plus more for sprinkling

½ teaspoon kosher salt

Freshly ground black pepper

3 hearts of romaine, coarsely chopped

2 ripe tomatoes, cut into chunks

2 Persian cucumbers, thickly sliced

½ cup pitted kalamata olives

1 cup thick-sliced Greek feta

2 scallions, chopped

1 lemon, cut into wedges

4 pitas, cut into wedges and warmed

HELPFUL TOOLS

Mason jar or whisk

1 In a mason jar, combine the olive oil, vinegar, garlic, oregano, salt, and a generous grinding of pepper. Secure the lid and shake vigorously. (Or you can whisk the ingredients together in a bowl.)

2 Arrange the romaine, tomatoes, cucumbers, olives, and sliced feta on a platter. Drizzle the dressing on top and garnish with the scallions and additional oregano. Serve with lemon wedges and warm pita on the side.

Recipe pictured on page 32

BIBB LETTUCE
with Shallot Vinaigrette

Truly, a simple salad at its finest. Since there aren't many ingredients, it's important to find the freshest lettuce you can, and use high-quality vinegar and mustard. These will come together and really shine. Serve the salad with something warm and savory, like hamburgers or roast chicken. *Serves 4*

2 teaspoons white wine vinegar

2 teaspoons Dijon mustard

1 shallot, minced

6 tablespoons extra virgin olive oil

Kosher salt and freshly ground black pepper

1 large head green Bibb lettuce, washed and torn into bite-size pieces

1 In a small bowl, whisk together the vinegar, mustard, and shallot. Gradually whisk in the olive oil to form an emulsion. Season with salt and pepper.

2 Place the lettuce in a large bowl, add the dressing, and toss. Season with salt and pepper and serve.

When you get toward the end of a jar of mustard, you can make the dressing in the jar. Just add all the ingredients to the mustard remaining in the jar, shake, and...voilà! Super easy to store, too.

TUNA SALAD TARTINES

Our dad told us that sometime in the late 1980s, canned Mediterranean tuna lost its popularity to seared ahi tuna. It was used in Niçoise salads and "fancy" sandwiches, much to his dismay. Here, we shine the spotlight back on canned tuna, which—according to Dad—is the best choice for Niçoise or tuna salad. Be sure to buy tuna packed in oil. *Serves 4*

2 (5-ounce) cans tuna packed in oil

½ cup small thinly sliced fennel bulb, plus fennel fronds for garnish

½ lemon, peeled, segmented into supremes (see box, page 11), and diced

¼ cup black olives, chopped

1 tablespoon small capers

4 slices whole grain bread, lightly toasted

8 leaves fresh basil, cut into thin strips

½ roasted red pepper, cut into long, thin strips

Extra virgin olive oil, for drizzling

Sea salt and freshly ground black pepper

HELPFUL TOOLS

Colander

1   Drain the tuna in a colander, then place in a bowl and lightly break into large chunks with your hands. Add the fennel, lemon pieces, olives, and capers. Toss to distribute the ingredients.

2   Lay the bread on a large cutting board and divide the tuna salad among the slices. Garnish with basil, roasted red pepper, and fennel fronds.

3   Drizzle the tartines with a little olive oil and season with sea salt and pepper. Cut into pieces and serve.

To roast a red pepper, place it on a gas burner or open flame, turning with tongs until charred all around. Then peel off the black bits and slice. This can also be store-bought.

Oven Roasted
Tomato Soup
PAGE 42

Cast Iron Grilled Cheese
PAGE 43

CAST IRON GRILLED CHEESE

Want to hear a secret? If you spread the *outside* of your sandwich with mayonnaise before making grilled cheese, you'll get the most delicious, savory crunch. Shhh—don't tell anyone! **Serves 4**

8 slices white bread

½ cup mayonnaise, preferably Hellmann's

8 slices mild cheddar cheese

HELPFUL TOOLS

Cast iron skillet

1   Heat a large cast iron skillet over medium-low heat.

2   Evenly spread one side of each bread slice with 1 tablespoon mayo.

3   Place four slices of bread in the pan, mayo-side down, and top each with two cheese slices. Top with the other slices of bread, mayo-side up. (Work in batches if your pan only fits two pieces of bread.)

4   Cook the sandwiches for a few minutes, until the bottom is golden brown, 4 to 5 minutes. Flip the sandwiches and cook for a few more minutes, until the other side is also golden brown and the cheese is melted. Cut in half and serve.

A panini press could be used instead of a skillet. Just be sure to build your entire sandwich before pressing.

OVEN ROASTED TOMATO SOUP

We couldn't offer our grilled cheese sandwich recipe without also including our best version of tomato soup. Taking the extra step of roasting the tomatoes deepens and expands the character of the soup. *Serves 4 to 5*

2 (28-ounce) cans whole tomatoes in juice, preferably San Marzano

½ cup extra virgin olive oil, divided, plus more for drizzling

1 yellow onion, finely diced

2 carrots, peeled and finely diced

2 celery stalks, peeled and finely diced

2 tablespoons sugar

2 tablespoons garlic salt

2 teaspoons crushed red pepper flakes

1 teaspoon celery salt

2 bay leaves

¼ cup fresh basil leaves, thinly sliced, for garnish

HELPFUL TOOLS

Sheet pan

Dutch oven or large pot

Immersion or regular blender

1   Preheat the oven to 300°F. Drain the tomatoes, saving the juice. Place the tomatoes on a foil-lined sheet pan and drizzle with olive oil. Roast for 2 hours, turning occasionally, until deep scarlet red in color.

2   In a Dutch oven or large soup pot, heat ¼ cup of the olive oil over medium heat. Add the onion, carrots, and celery and sauté until softened, about 10 minutes.

3   Add the roasted tomatoes, reserved tomato juice, remaining ¼ cup olive oil, sugar, garlic salt, pepper flakes, celery salt, and bay leaves. Simmer for about 30 minutes to thicken, stirring occasionally. Let cool for about 5 minutes. Remove and discard the bay leaves. Puree the soup in the pot with an immersion blender until smooth, or transfer to a regular blender and puree.

4   Serve with an additional drizzle of olive oil and fresh basil leaves.

 Be careful putting hot liquids in a blender. At the start, pulse and then let out the steam to release any pressure that could build up inside.

Recipe pictured on page 40

SHORT STACK TURKEY CLUB

Although a club sandwich is crave-worthy, it's nearly impossible to eat. To solve, we came up with a short stack version, which has all the traditional flavors of the sandwich but is much easier to handle or take along with you. Our amped-up mayo and trick for keeping the bread dry takes the sandwich to the next level. This is one of our top picks for weekend eating on the golf course or sports field!

Serves 4

½ cup mayonnaise, preferably Hellmann's

1 tablespoon chopped fresh tarragon

1 tablespoon chopped fresh basil

1 tablespoon chopped fresh parsley

1 teaspoon minced garlic

8 slices white bread, lightly toasted

1 head Bibb lettuce

8 slices ripe tomato

8 slices thin bacon, cooked until crisp

12 slices thinly sliced oven roasted turkey

Potato chips, for serving

HELPFUL TOOLS

Serrated knife

1   In a small bowl, combine the mayonnaise, herbs, and garlic.

2   Spread 1 tablespoon of the mayo mixture on one side of each slice of bread, crust to crust.

3   To build the sandwiches, layer the ingredients on four slices in the following order: Place one piece of lettuce, then two slices of tomato side by side, another piece of lettuce, two slices of bacon, and then finally, the turkey.

4   Top each sandwich with another slice of bread, mayo-side down. Cut the sandwiches in half with a serrated knife and serve with your favorite potato chips.

PARISIAN HAM SANDWICH

We've been lucky enough to visit France a few times, and during our first visit, we fell in love with *jambon beurre,* French for ham and butter sandwich. ***Serves 2 to 4***

1 French baguette, fresh from the bakery

4 tablespoons salted butter, softened

12 slices thinly sliced French ham or smoked ham

Cornichons to serve alongside

Serrated knife

1   Slice the baguette lengthwise with a serrated knife.

2   Spread the softened butter on the cut surfaces of the bread, dividing it equally between top and bottom.

3   Layer the ham on the butter. Replace top of baguette.

4   Cut the sandwich into four pieces and serve with cornichons on the side.

Variations

· Use small baguettes to make mini versions of the sandwich.

· Slice the cornichons and put them inside the sandwich.

CHILLED CORN SOUP

Synonymous with summer sunshine, corn soup in August is one of our family traditions for picnicking. It travels well in a thermos, and it's such a cool contrast to the usual picnic foods. *Serves 4 to 6*

2 tablespoons unsalted butter

½ small yellow onion, cut into medium dice

1 small garlic clove, sliced

1 bay leaf

1 fresh tarragon sprig

4 ears fresh sweet corn on the cob, kernels removed

1 teaspoon kosher salt, plus more for seasoning

1 cup water

2 tablespoons extra virgin olive oil

Grated zest and juice of 1 lime

¼ cup lump crab meat, shredded

2 teaspoons minced cilantro

2 teaspoons minced chives

Lime wedges, for serving

HELPFUL TOOLS

Microplane zester

Dutch oven or large pot

Regular blender or immersion blender

Ladle

1   Melt the butter in a Dutch oven or large soup pot over low to medium heat. Add the onion and garlic and cook until soft. Add the bay leaf and tarragon and continue to cook for 2 minutes. Add the corn kernels, salt, and water.

2   Cook for 40 minutes, or until soup has thickened and reduced a bit. Remove from the heat.

3   Discard the tarragon and bay leaf. Working in batches, blend the soup in a blender until smooth, drizzling in the olive oil as it blends. (Or you can blend the soup in the pot with an immersion blender.) Season with salt and the lime juice. Refrigerate until chilled, about 1 hour.

4   In a small bowl, mix together the crab meat, cilantro, chives, and lime zest. Garnish each bowl with a small amount of this mixture and ladle soup around the garnish and serve with a lime wedge.

TIPS

You can save the corn cobs and add them to the soup while it is cooking for extra flavor. Discard them before blending.

Be careful with hot liquids in a blender (see page 42).

BUTTERNUT SQUASH & APPLE SOUP

We enjoy this cold-weather soup every year, all the way from Thanksgiving through to the end of February, often by the fire. For parties, we prepare the soup ahead of time, and then we put on a big pot for guests to help themselves. This keeps the mess in the kitchen low and gives us something yummy to sneak off with and eat. *Serves 4*

4 tablespoons unsalted butter

1 large butternut squash, peeled and cubed (about 4 cups)

1 medium yellow onion, chopped

2 tart apples, peeled, cored, and cubed

1 tablespoon Madras curry powder

¼ cup all-purpose flour

3 cups chicken broth

½ cup half-and-half

Kosher salt and freshly ground black pepper

¼ cup toasted pine nuts, for garnish

HELPFUL TOOLS

Immersion blender or regular blender

1 Melt the butter in a large soup or stockpot over medium heat. Add the squash, onion, apples, and curry powder and sauté for 5 minutes.

2 Add the flour, stirring well to combine. Add the broth, bring to a simmer, and simmer for 30 minutes, or until squash is very tender. Let cool for a few minutes.

3 With an immersion blender, puree the soup in the pot until smooth. Alternatively, carefully puree in batches in a regular blender. Stir in the half-and-half.

4 Reheat soup gently if necessary and season with salt and pepper. Garnish with toasted pine nuts and serve.

TIPS

Pine nuts can be toasted in a pan on the stovetop or roasted on a sheet pan in a 325°F oven for 12 minutes. Give a little shake as they cook. Watch them carefully, because they can burn quickly!

If using a regular blender, be careful with hot liquids (see page 42).

GRANDMA'S CHICKEN NOODLE SOUP

Our grandmother Marie has been making this soup for decades. We love her, and we absolutely love cooking with her, so of course we love the soup, too! Try it yourself, or even more importantly, take time to learn a tried-and-true recipe from someone in *your* family. Generational cooking is one of the most special things to do together in the kitchen. *Serves 6 to 8*

1 whole organic chicken, 3 to 4 pounds

1 tablespoon kosher salt, plus more for seasoning, and freshly ground black pepper

2 chicken bouillon cubes

1 large yellow or white onion, chopped finely

6 stalks celery, chopped and divided

6 carrots, peeled, chopped and divided

8 sprigs fresh parsley, plus ¼ cup chopped parsley for garnish

Cooked egg noodles, kept warm or at room temperature

HELPFUL TOOLS

Fine-mesh strainer

Ladle

1   Rinse the chicken under cold water. Place the chicken in a large soup pot or stockpot and add enough cold water to cover. Place the pot over high heat and bring to a boil. Remove from the heat, drain the chicken in a colander, and rinse the chicken well. Return the chicken to the pot and cover with fresh cold water.

2   Bring to a boil again, then reduce the heat to a simmer. Add the salt, pepper, and bouillon. Simmer for about 1 hour, or until the chicken is falling off the bone.

3   Remove the chicken from the pot and set aside to cool. Add onion, celery, carrots, and parsley to the broth. Season again with salt and pepper. Simmer until vegetables are tender, approximately 12 to 15 minutes. Remove parsley sprigs and discard.

4   While vegetables are cooking and chicken is cool enough to handle, shred and pull the meat from the bones. Once vegetables are cooked, return the chicken meat to the broth. Stir and shut off the heat.

5   Place the cooked egg noodles in the bottom of serving bowls and ladle the soup over the top. Garnish with chopped parsley and serve.

CRAZY POPCORN SOUP

Popcorn in soup? You're probably thinking that's nuts! But it's delicious and truly unique. Just make sure to strain the soup as noted below. It's an important step that removes all the small bits of kernel so you've got a velvety end result. **Serves 4**

3 tablespoons unsalted butter

2 medium leeks (white and light green parts), thinly sliced and well rinsed

2 cloves garlic, chopped

1 tablespoon peeled chopped fresh ginger

2 teaspoons Madras curry powder

2½ cups plain popped popcorn, divided

1 quart chicken stock

1 cup canned pumpkin puree

¾ cup full-fat coconut milk

Juice of 1 lime (about 2 tablespoons)

Kosher salt

HELPFUL TOOLS

Regular blender or immersion blender

Fine-mesh strainer

1 In a medium saucepan, melt the butter over medium heat. Add the leeks and cook until wilted, about 5 minutes. Add the garlic, ginger, and curry powder and cook, stirring, until fragrant, about 1 minute. Add 2 cups of the popcorn and toss to coat in the butter.

2 Add the stock, pumpkin puree, and coconut milk. Bring to a simmer and cook until the leeks are very tender, the popcorn has dissolved away from the kernels, and the kernels are softened, about 30 minutes. Remove from the heat.

3 Puree the soup with an immersion blender in the pot, or in batches in a regular blender. Working in batches, strain the soup through a fine-mesh strainer to remove the popcorn kernels. Stir in the lime juice and taste for seasoning, adding a little salt if necessary. Serve the soup in individual bowls with the remaining popcorn as a garnish.

 Be careful with hot liquids in a blender (see page 42).

GAME DAY PORK CHILI

This is the Zakarian TV dinner! Whenever there's something fun to watch, we make a batch of chili and all gather in the living room. This is the absolute *only* time we're allowed to eat dinner in front of the TV, so chili holds an extra special place in our hearts. **Serves 8**

3 tablespoons extra virgin olive oil

3 pounds ground pork

2 to 3 tablespoons pancetta or bacon, cut into small pieces

Kosher salt and freshly ground black pepper

2 large onions, chopped (about 3 cups)

6 garlic cloves, finely chopped

2 bunches scallions (white and green parts), chopped (about 2 cups)

2 tablespoons tomato paste

¼ cup chili powder

¼ cup ground cumin

1½ cups apple cider

2 (28-ounce) cans whole tomatoes with juice (fire-roasted tomatoes if you can find them), crushed by hand

2 (15.5-ounce) cans small black or white beans, drained and rinsed

2 cups chicken stock

2 tablespoons green Tabasco

1 avocado, pitted, peeled, and chopped, for garnish

½ cup chopped cilantro, for garnish

4 radishes, sliced thin, for garnish

Shredded Mexican cheese, for garnish

Lime wedges, for garnish

HELPFUL TOOLS

Wide-bottomed Dutch oven or large pot

Wooden or silicone spurtle (see page xv), or a wooden spoon

Ladle

1   Heat the olive oil in a wide-bottomed Dutch oven or large soup pot over medium-high heat. Add the pork and cook, stirring and scraping the pan bottom with a spurtle, until browned and cooked through, letting the liquid cook out. This will take 10 to 15 minutes. Caution: Do not rush through this step; it's crucial. Add the pancetta or bacon and cook with the pork for 1 to 2 minutes. Season with pepper, about 1 teaspoon.

2   Reduce the heat to medium. Add the onions, garlic, and scallions and cook until wilted, about 5 minutes. Make a space in the pan and drop in the tomato paste. Let the paste toast for 1 minute and then stir it into the pork mixture. Sprinkle in the chili powder and cumin and cook and stir until fragrant, about 2 minutes.

3   Pour in the cider, rigorously scraping the bottom of the pan with the spurtle to get the brown bits released and incorporated. Cook until the liquid is almost reduced away, 3 to 5 minutes. Add the tomatoes, beans, and stock, then season with the Tabasco as well as about 2 tablespoons salt and 1 tablespoon pepper. Adjust the heat so the chili is gently simmering and cook, uncovered, until the chili is thick and full of character, about 1½ hours.

4   Ladle the chili into bowls and serve garnished with avocado, cilantro, radishes, Mexican cheese, and lime wedges.

Serve this along with chips, crudités, and dips to make it a complete "snacking" meal.

MAIN COURSES

CACIO E PEPE

Cacio e pepe, spoken as *ka-chee-oh e pep-ey*, is translated from Italian to English as "cheese and pepper." Upon seeing this dish for the first time, we decidedly did not like it. Life tip: Snap judgments are often ill conceived. Luckily, we tasted it and fell in love. It's quite simple and makes for a quick and easy weeknight dinner. ***Serves 4 to 5***

Kosher salt

12 ounces thick-cut dry pasta, such as pappardelle

30 turns freshly ground black pepper (on the coarsest setting), plus more for serving

⅓ cup grated pecorino Romano cheese, plus more for serving

3 tablespoons extra virgin olive oil, plus more for drizzling

HELPFUL TOOLS

Pepper mill

1　Fill a pan just wide enough to hold the pasta with 1 inch of water. Season the water with a pinch of salt and bring to a boil. Spread the pasta in the pan and cook over medium-high heat, stirring occasionally to prevent the pasta from sticking together. You want to cook the pasta, while allowing the water to reduce. Do not add more water, as you want the starchy water to be minimal when the remaining ingredients are added. Once the pasta is al dente, about 9 to 11 minutes in the boiling water, and the pasta water has reduced so only a slight coating remains at the bottom of the pan, turn off the heat.

2　Meanwhile, toast the pepper in a small pan over medium heat until fragrant, 1 to 2 minutes.

3　Add the toasted pepper and pecorino to the pasta. Stir and toss vigorously until both ingredients are well incorporated into the pasta. Toss in the olive oil and season with salt.

4　Transfer the pasta to a large bowl and garnish with more black pepper, pecorino, and olive oil.

Recipe pictured on page 63

RISOTTO 3X

We beg you not to be scared off by making risotto. It's truly not hard. It just takes a little attention. To get your head around it, think of it this way: The method is a simple process of adding liquid to rice and then cooking it off three times in a row. You can do it! *Serves 6*

6 cups chicken stock

¾ cup extra virgin olive oil, divided

1 small Spanish onion, finely diced

Kosher salt and freshly ground black pepper

12 ounces carnaroli or arborio rice

½ cup white wine

½ cup grated Parmesan cheese

6 tablespoons (¾ stick) of unsalted butter or 3 ounces truffle butter

¼ cup minced chives, optional

HELPFUL TOOLS

Silicone spatula or wooden spoon

Ladle

1   In a medium saucepan, bring the stock to a simmer over medium heat. Then keep at a low simmer over low heat.

2   In a large sauté pan, heat ¼ cup of the olive oil over medium heat. Add the onion and cook, stirring occasionally, until translucent, about 6 minutes. Season with salt and pepper.

3   Add the rice and turn the heat to medium-high. Cook, stirring the rice continuously and allowing it to lightly toast, for about 2 minutes. Add the wine and scrape the bottom of the pan with a silicone spatula or wooden spoon to prevent the rice from sticking. Cook until the wine has completely evaporated, then return the heat to medium.

4   Add a ladle of the simmering stock, enough to just come to the surface of the rice, and cook, stirring occasionally, until evaporated. Repeat this process twice more, stirring the rice a bit with each addition. On the third time, the grains should be al dente and the entire mixture a bit creamy. This should take about 18 minutes. If not ready, go one more round with a full or half ladle of stock.

5   Add the Parmesan, turn the heat off, and emulsify the butter and remaining ½ cup olive oil by vigorously stirring them into the rice using the spatula. Fold in the chives (if using), and re-season with salt and pepper if needed. Serve immediately.

Recipe pictured on page 62

CLOCKWISE FROM TOP OF TABLE AT LEFT: Cacio e Pepe, *page 60*; GZ's Spaghetti Bolognese, *page 66*; Risotto 3X, *page 61*; Linguine with Fresh Clams, *page 67*; Classic Meatballs with Garlic Bread, *page 64*

CLASSIC MEATBALLS
with Garlic Bread

There are a couple of important tips for this recipe: 1) use a high-quality mix of ground pork, veal, and beef for the meatballs; and 2) don't overmix, otherwise the meatballs will have a meatloaf-type consistency. A fun variation is meatball soup: Make mini meatballs with the recipe, then add them to our Grandma's Chicken Noodle Soup (page 53), along with a (28-ounce) can of Italian peeled tomatoes that you can crush in the pot with a wooden spoon, and there you go! As for the garlic bread, you can of course include it with just about any pasta meal, but it also works as a warm, pre-meal bruschetta if you cut it into small pieces and then top them with fresh diced tomatoes. *Serves 4 to 6*

FOR THE MEATBALLS

1 large onion, cut into chunks

3 garlic cloves, peeled

1 cup water

½ pound ground pork

½ pound ground veal

½ pound ground beef

3 large eggs

½ cup grated Parmesan cheese, plus more for serving

1 cup unseasoned dried bread crumbs

¼ cup chopped fresh Italian parsley

Pinch of red pepper flakes

Kosher salt and freshly ground black pepper

Extra virgin olive oil, for drizzling

1 To make the meatballs: In a food processor, combine the onion, garlic, and water. Puree until very smooth.

2 In a large mixing bowl, combine the pork, veal, beef, eggs, Parmesan, bread crumbs, parsley, red pepper flakes, and salt and pepper to taste. Add the onion puree and, with your hands, mix until just combined.

3 Wet your hands and form the mixture into 24 meatballs, placing them on a sheet pan. Drizzle the meatballs with olive oil.

1 loaf French bread

8 tablespoons (1 stick) salted butter, softened

½ cup grated Parmesan cheese

3 garlic cloves, minced

½ cup roughly chopped fresh parsley

1 teaspoon chopped fresh rosemary

1 teaspoon chopped fresh thyme

¼ teaspoon garlic powder

HELPFUL TOOLS

Food processor

Sheet pans

Parchment paper

Meat thermometer

4   To make the garlic bread: Cut the bread loaf lengthwise in half and place on a sheet pan lined with parchment paper. In a small bowl, combine the softened butter, Parmesan, minced garlic, parsley, rosemary, thyme, and garlic powder. Spread evenly on each cut side of the bread. Set aside.

5   Preheat the oven to 375°F. Bake the meatballs on the bottom rack for 25 to 30 minutes, until a thermometer registers 160°F when inserted into a meatball. Halfway through baking, place the garlic bread on the top rack and bake until toasted. Place the garlic bread on a cutting board, slice into eight pieces, and serve warm with the meatballs.

Recipe pictured on page 63

GZ'S SPAGHETTI BOLOGNESE

Spaghetti Bolognese is a well-rounded dinner choice because it puts protein, vegetables, and starch all on one plate. There are so many versions of Bolognese sauce made with endless additions and secret ingredients. This recipe below is the purest, yummiest version, we guarantee you. This is because our dad became obsessed with trying out every Bolognese recipe he could get his hands on… and then he came up with his own. We give it a gold star every time! **Serves 6 to 8**

¼ cup extra virgin olive oil

1½ pounds ground chuck

1½ pounds ground veal

½ pound Italian sausage meat

2 yellow onions, chopped

2 carrots, peeled and chopped

6 garlic cloves, sliced

½ cup tomato paste

1 cup red wine

2 cups beef stock

2 (28-ounce) cans San Marzano tomatoes, crushed

1 sprig fresh thyme and 3 sprigs fresh rosemary, tied together with string

3-inch chunk pecorino Romano cheese rind

12 ounces spaghetti, cooked

Shaved pecorino Romano cheese, for serving

HELPFUL TOOLS

Dutch oven or large pot

Food processor

Wooden spatula

1 Heat the olive oil in a Dutch oven or large pot over high heat. Add the chuck, veal, and sausage and cook until well browned. Remove the meat with a slotted spoon and set aside on a plate, keeping the fat in the pot.

2 Process the onions, carrots, and garlic in a food processor until the size of small pebbles. Add to the fat in the pot and sweat over medium heat until very soft and lightly browned, about 10 minutes. Return the meat mixture and any juices on the plate to the pot. Add the tomato paste and cook, stirring occasionally, for about 10 minutes.

3 Add the wine and scrape the bottom of the pot with a wooden spatula to remove bits that have adhered to the pot. Continue cooking over medium heat until the liquid is reduced by half. Add the stock, tomatoes, thyme and rosemary bundle, and pecorino rind. Cover and simmer slowly over low heat for about 1 hour and 30 minutes, until the sauce is thickened and reduced.

4 Lightly coat the freshly cooked spaghetti with Bolognese sauce and pass shaved pecorino Romano cheese at the table. You can top your pasta with more sauce if you prefer.

We do have one secret ingredient we couldn't help but share: To really go pro, add a tablespoon of dried porcini powder when you add the wine.

Recipe pictured on page 62

LINGUINI
with Fresh Clams

When you travel, it's great to learn about new foods. Beforehand, try researching local spots, so you don't waste your time in touristy restaurants. We tried linguini with clams, known in Italian as *vongole*, for the first time in Naples, Italy, at a small, authentic restaurant called Da Dora, located down a dark side street. The sense of mystery ran as high as our nerves as we walked down the street and through the porthole doors. An Italian seafood restaurant in a new city down a strange dark alley?! Yikes! But it was filled with locals, so we decided to go with the flow and took a leap of faith. We're so glad we did. We remember it as one of the best pastas we've ever eaten. The gift of travel expands the palate...we hope to find our way back to Da Dora one day. ***Serves 4***

12 ounces dried linguini

Kosher salt

4 tablespoons unsalted butter

2 tablespoons extra virgin olive oil

6 cloves garlic, finely chopped

1 tablespoon Calabrian chili paste

¾ cup dry white wine

½ cup clam juice

Freshly ground black pepper

2 pounds littleneck clams, scrubbed

¼ cup chopped fresh parsley, plus more for garnish

Grated zest and juice of 1 lemon

HELPFUL TOOLS
Microplane zester

1   Cook the pasta in a large pot of salted boiling water until al dente. Drain, keeping just a bit of the cooking water, and return the pasta to the pot and keep warm.

2   Meanwhile, in a large skillet over medium heat, heat the butter and olive oil. When the butter has melted, add the garlic and chili paste and cook until the garlic is fragrant, about 60 seconds. Add the wine, clam juice, and pepper to taste, increase the heat slightly, and cook until bubbling, about 2 minutes. Add the clams and increase the heat. Cover and cook just until the clams open, 3 to 5 minutes. If any clams don't open, throw them away. Taste the sauce and adjust salt and pepper as needed.

3   Add the pasta to the sauce and warm through over medium heat. Toss in the parsley, lemon zest, and lemon juice. Portion into individual bowls and garnish with extra parsley.

Recipe pictured on page 63

STEAMED HALIBUT
with Coconut Rice

Our mom came up with this recipe as a light, healthy meal for us. She likes serving fish for the obvious reasons, and we (our little brother, George, included) like eating it because of the coconut rice. This is what we call a win-win—for us, *and* for Mom! *Serves 4*

FOR THE HALIBUT

4 (6-ounce) halibut fillets, skin removed

Kosher salt and freshly ground black pepper

1 teaspoon grated fresh ginger

4 scallions, thinly sliced

2 teaspoons toasted sesame oil

2 lemons, cut into 8 slices

FOR THE COCONUT RICE

1 cup jasmine rice

1 cup water

1 cup full-fat coconut milk

½ teaspoon kosher salt

HELPFUL TOOLS

Parchment paper

Wide spatula

1 To make the halibut: Preheat the oven to 400°F. Lay out four 9x11-inch sheets of parchment paper on a flat surface. Season the halibut fillets generously with salt and pepper, then place one near the bottom edge of each piece of parchment. Evenly divide the ginger, scallions, sesame oil, and lemon slices and place on top of each halibut piece. Fold the top half of the parchment over to meet the bottom. Crimp the edges together tightly in ¼-inch folds to create a closed packet with the fish inside and place on a sheet pan. (This is called "en papillote"—a good method to learn by watching online videos.)

2 To make the rice: In a medium saucepan, combine the rice, water, coconut milk, and salt. Bring to a boil, then cover and reduce the heat to low. Cook rice, according to its package instructions, until liquid is absorbed. Uncover and fluff with a fork.

3 While the rice is cooking, place the sheet pan with the halibut packets in the oven and bake for 10 to 12 minutes. Remove from the oven and carefully cut open the packets, allowing steam to escape. With a wide spatula, place a piece of halibut on each plate, pouring juices from their packets over the tops. Serve with the coconut rice.

SHRIMP SCAMPI

Truth be told, Shrimp Scampi is actually a misnomer, as *scampi* simply means "shrimp" in Italian. With full translation, the above heading is essentially "Shrimp Shrimps." It's a hilarious Americanism, so we're happy to help this funny recipe name live on. On a more serious note, this is one of the most satisfying seafood dishes of all time. *Serves 6 to 8*

8 tablespoons (1 stick) unsalted butter, at room temperature

2 teaspoons chopped fresh Italian parsley, plus more for garnish

2 teaspoons chopped fresh tarragon, plus more for garnish

2 pounds extra-large shrimp, peeled (tail shells left on) and butterflied

Kosher salt and freshly ground black pepper

2 tablespoons all-purpose flour, for dusting

Extra virgin olive oil

4 cloves garlic, minced

¾ cup dry white wine

6 tablespoons fresh lemon juice (from 2 lemons)

¼ cup chicken stock

1 pound spaghetti, cooked al dente

1 loaf of crusty bread

1   Combine the butter, parsley, and tarragon in a bowl and mix with a fork until well combined. Transfer the butter to a sheet of plastic wrap and form into a 1-inch log. Enclose the log in the plastic wrap, then refrigerate until it is thoroughly chilled.

2   Pat the shrimp dry, season with salt and pepper, and lightly dust with flour. Heat 2 tablespoons olive oil in a large skillet over medium-high heat. Working in three or four batches, add only as many shrimp that fit in the pan in a single, uncrowded layer. Cook the shrimp, turning so they are golden on both sides and nearly cooked through, about 3 minutes per batch. Add more oil to your pan when it starts to look dry. Transfer the shrimp to a large plate lined with paper towels to drain any excess oil.

3   Once the shrimp are cooked, wipe the pan clean. Add about 1 tablespoon olive oil and adjust the heat to medium-low. Add the garlic and cook, stirring frequently, until it is soft and fragrant, about 1 minute. Add the wine, lemon juice, and stock, raise the heat to medium, and bring to a simmer. Cook the sauce until it is reduced by about two-thirds, 4 to 5 minutes. Taste and season with salt and pepper if necessary.

4   Cut the chilled herb butter into small pieces and whisk it into the sauce one piece at a time. Season the sauce with salt and pepper to taste. Return the shrimp to the pan and cook, stirring, until heated through and well coated with sauce.

5   Place the cooked spaghetti in a large serving bowl. Top with the shrimp and sauce, then toss to coat. Garnish with additional chopped parsley and tarragon and serve immediately with crusty bread.

TIP   *If you want to serve the shrimp by itself, just double the recipe and forget the pasta.*

CRISPY SKIN SALMON
with Herb Butter

There's one thing that makes this dish extra special: the crispy skin. So make sure that once you place the fillets skin side down in the pan, you don't touch them for 5 minutes. You'll be tempted, we know, but resist! However, you can take a peek to make sure they're golden on the edges before turning and putting the salmon in the oven. *Serves 4*

4 tablespoons unsalted butter, softened

1 clove garlic, minced

1 tablespoon minced fresh tarragon

1 tablespoon minced fresh parsley

1 tablespoon minced fresh thyme

Grated zest of 1 lemon

2 tablespoons canola oil

4 skin-on center-cut salmon fillets (each about 6 ounces)

Kosher salt

HELPFUL TOOLS

Microplane zester

Cast iron or ovenproof skillet

1 Preheat the oven to 375°F. In a small bowl, mix together the butter, garlic, tarragon, parsley, thyme, and lemon zest. Set aside.

2 Heat the oil over medium-high heat in a cast iron or other ovenproof skillet. Season the salmon with salt and place, skin side down, in the pan. Cook for about 5 minutes to crisp up the skin.

3 Remove the pan from heat and turn the fillets over. Divide the herb butter mixture among the four fillets, using a spatula to coat evenly.

4 Transfer the pan to the oven and roast the salmon for 7 to 10 minutes, until the centers of the fillets are almost done but a little pink remains. Season with a touch of salt and serve immediately.

Before placing the salmon in the pan, drag the back edge of a knife with some force along the skin to push some water and moisture out. This will help get the skin nice and crispy.

WHOLE BRANZINO
with Braised Fennel

Roasting an entire fish at home might sound like a lot to handle, but once you try it, you'll see how easy, foolproof, and rewarding it can be. The photograph here shows what it should look like each step of the way: raw, roasted, and filleted. Find a reliable fishmonger and have them gut and clean the fish for you. Two tips about the eyes: 1) When you buy the fish, check to make sure the eyes are very clear in color to ensure freshness. 2) You know the fish is cooked the moment the eyes turn white. *Serves 4*

4 whole branzino, gutted and cleaned, head and tail left intact

1½ tablespoons kosher salt

Freshly ground black pepper

2 lemons, thinly sliced

8 fresh parsley sprigs

1 head of fennel

1 star anise

¼ cup extra virgin olive oil, plus more for drizzling

1 sprig fresh thyme

1 clove garlic, peeled

Canola oil

Fresh watercress, for serving

Balsamic vinegar, for drizzling

HELPFUL TOOLS

Sheet pans

Parchment paper

Butcher's twine

Cast iron grill pan

1 Lay the whole branzino on two parchment-lined sheet pans, two fish per pan. Season inside the cavities with salt and freshly cracked pepper. Place three slices of lemon and two sprigs of parsley in the cavity of each fish. Tie each fish in two spots with the butcher's twine, one one-third from the tail, the other one-third from the head. Refrigerate until you are ready to cook it.

2 Cut the fennel into eight pieces from top to bottom, ensuring that each piece has a little bit of the core so that they remain intact. Place the fennel in a medium saucepan and add enough water to cover. Add the star anise, olive oil, thyme, and garlic and cover with lid. Simmer over low heat, checking every couple of minutes, until the fennel is tender, about 8 to 10 minutes. Remove from heat and set aside.

3 Heat a grill pan over medium-high heat. Brush the branzino with canola oil, then season the interior and exterior with salt and pepper. Working in batches, place the fish on the grill pan and cook without moving for 5 to 7 minutes, until pronounced grill marks develop. Flip the fish and cook until the fish is cooked through, about 2 minutes.

4 While the branzino cooks, heat 2 tablespoons canola oil in a sauté pan. Season the fennel with salt and pepper to taste. Cook until the fennel gets a touch of color around the edges, about 1 minute.

5 To assemble the dish, remove the twine from the fish and discard the lemon slices and parsley sprigs from the cavities. Place the grilled fish on a platter with the roasted fennel. Garnish with watercress, drizzle with balsamic vinegar and olive oil, and serve.

Should you wish to fillet the fish, we recommend watching an online video demonstration: How to Fillet a Cooked Whole Branzino.

BUILD-YOUR-OWN FISH TACOS

We like to make so many types of tacos that it was hard to choose just one to include here. In this recipe, we mix up the seasoning a bit to give the cod a little extra kick. Feel free to go more or less with any of the spices below. Or to keep it really easy, you can season the cod simply before roasting with just salt, pepper, oregano, and lemon zest. Have fun! *Serves 4*

1 tablespoon chili powder

1 teaspoon ground cumin

1 teaspoon garlic powder

1 teaspoon onion powder

1 teaspoon paprika

2 teaspoons kosher salt

1½ pounds fresh cod fillets

1 tablespoon extra virgin olive oil

8 (6-inch) corn or flour tortillas

1 avocado, pitted, peeled, and sliced

¼ cup minced cilantro, for garnish

1 cup shredded purple cabbage

1 lime, cut into wedges

HELPFUL TOOLS

Sheet pan

Tongs

1 Preheat the oven to 400°F. Combine the chili powder, cumin, garlic powder, onion powder, paprika, and salt in a medium bowl.

2 Place the cod on a foil-lined sheet pan and rub generously on both sides with the spice mixture. Drizzle with the olive oil.

3 Bake for 12 to 15 minutes, until the fish is flaky and cooked through. Remove from the oven.

4 In a large skillet or directly over a gas burner at medium heat, warm the tortillas briefly, flipping once with tongs. Place on plates.

5 Break the fish into large chunks and divide among the tortillas. Top with the avocado slices, cilantro, and cabbage and serve with lime wedges.

Recipe pictured on page 78

Build-Your-Own Fish Tacos
PAGE 76

HONEY MUSTARD CHICKEN SKEWERS

Traditional chicken fingers are a beloved option that's hard to resist, but if you're looking to give them a rest, this recipe is just as satisfying. We love to have these with Fragrant Rice Pilaf (page 101) and Mediterranean Cauliflower (page 95) for a full meal. *Serves 6*

½ cup Dijon mustard

¼ cup honey

¼ cup plain whole-milk Greek yogurt

2 tablespoons extra virgin olive oil

¼ cup chopped fresh cilantro

1 (1-inch) piece fresh ginger, peeled and grated

½ teaspoon ground allspice

Kosher salt and freshly ground black pepper

2¼ pounds skinless, boneless chicken breast halves (about 6 small)

2 tablespoons chopped fresh parsley

1 teaspoon sesame seeds, toasted

HELPFUL TOOLS

Wooden or metal skewers

Grill, cast iron grill pan, or fry pan

Nonstick cooking spray

1   If using wooden skewers, soak for 15 to 30 minutes in water. Remove from the water and pat dry. (This is to prevent the wood from burning when on the grill.)

2   Combine the mustard, honey, yogurt, olive oil, cilantro, ginger, allspice, salt, and pepper in a large zip-top plastic bag. Cut each chicken breast into six cubes. Add the chicken to the bag; seal, turning to coat. Marinate, turning the bag occasionally, for at least 30 minutes at room temperature, or up to 2 hours in the fridge.

3   Spray the grill or grill pan with nonstick cooking spray and preheat to medium-high.

4   Remove the chicken from the bag, discarding marinade. Thread the chicken evenly onto 12 skewers. Grill, turning to cook evenly, for 10 minutes, or until cooked through (internal temperature of 155°F). Place the skewers on a platter, sprinkle with parsley and sesame seeds, and serve.

If you don't have a grill or grill pan, the chicken pieces can be cooked un-skewered, right in a fry pan.

ROASTED SPATCHCOCK CHICKEN

A spatchcock chicken might sound weird, but it's simply a chicken that has had its backbone removed. This allows it to open up and lie flat when the breast side is up. Cooking the chicken this way is a nice change from traditional roasting, and we've found that it goes faster, too, which is much appreciated, especially on a school night. Just ask your butcher to spatchcock the chicken for you. **Serves 4**

1 (3½-pound) whole spatchcock chicken

2 tablespoons extra virgin olive oil, divided

Kosher salt and freshly ground black pepper

2 heads garlic, cut in half horizontally

4 sprigs fresh rosemary

4 sprigs fresh thyme

1 lemon, cut in half horizontally

HELPFUL TOOLS

Large cast iron or ovenproof skillet

Meat thermometer

Tongs

1   Preheat the oven to 400°F. Rinse the chicken, pat dry, and rub all over with 1 tablespoon of the olive oil. Generously season on both sides with salt and pepper.

2   Heat a large cast iron or other ovenproof skillet over medium-high heat. Add the remaining 1 tablespoon olive oil. When the oil is hot, place the chicken, skin side down, in the pan. Cook until the skin starts to crisp on the edges and the color is golden brown. Flip the chicken over with tongs, taking care not to splatter oil toward yourself, and add the garlic, rosemary, and thyme around the chicken in the pan. Squeeze a lemon half over the top and place the other half in the pan, cut side down.

3   Transfer the pan to the oven and roast the chicken (skin side up) for 30 to 35 minutes, until a meat thermometer registers 155°F when inserted in the thickest part of a breast. Let rest for about 10 minutes, then carve and serve with pan juices.

CRISPY PORK MILANESE
with Arugula Tomato Salad

One of our top-five, all-time favorite dishes when eating out is Milanese, but you can make it at home, too! It's simple, and chicken or veal can be subbed in for pork. *Serves 4*

2 tablespoons fresh lemon juice

1 clove garlic, minced

Kosher salt and freshly ground black pepper

½ cup extra virgin olive oil, divided

3 cups arugula

1 cup cherry tomatoes, halved

1 red onion, thinly sliced

4 fresh basil leaves, sliced thin

4 boneless pork chops, ½ inch thick, about 6 ounces each

2 cups all-purpose flour

2 large eggs, whisked

2 cups panko bread crumbs

½ cup grated Parmesan cheese

HELPFUL TOOLS

Meat mallet

Sheet pan with optional rack

1   In a small bowl, combine the lemon juice, garlic, and 1 teaspoon salt. Whisk in ¼ cup of the olive oil to make the dressing. Place the arugula, tomatoes, onion, and basil in a large bowl. Reserve the salad and dressing in the refrigerator separately.

2   Working one at a time, place a pork chop in a gallon-size zip-top bag, leaving partially unsealed. With a meat mallet, pound the pork until about ¼ inch thick.

3   Place the flour, eggs, and panko separately in three medium bowls. Stir the Parmesan into the panko. Working one at a time, dredge the pork chops first in the flour, then the egg, and then coat in crumb mixture. Set aside on a plate.

4   Heat a large skillet over medium heat and add the remaining ¼ cup olive oil. When hot, add the pork and cook for about 5 minutes on each side, until golden brown. Transfer from the skillet to a sheet pan lined with a rack or paper towels. Season with salt and pepper. Dress the salad and plate immediately with the pork.

To make a big impression, ask your butcher to keep the loin bone in your pork or veal chops, as it makes for a nice presentation. If you go for this, just make sure that, when pounding, you get close to the bone. That way, the meat nearest the bone is equally as thin as the rest.

BISTRO HANGER STEAK
with Caramelized Shallots

Hanger steak is a tender and delicious steak choice that happens to be more economical than many other cuts, like tenderloin or rib eye. For any steak, it's crucial that it's at room temperature before you start, so it cooks evenly throughout. Also, when seasoning before cooking, use more salt and pepper than you think is needed on all sides of the meat. Seasoning raw meat like this takes some getting used to, but doing it is more than half the skill used in this dish. *Serves 2 to 4*

FOR THE STEAK

1 teaspoon celery salt

1 teaspoon sugar

1 teaspoon freshly ground black pepper

¼ teaspoon cayenne pepper

1 hanger steak (about 1¾ pounds); ask the butcher to remove the center sinew

2 tablespoons extra virgin olive oil

FOR THE CARAMELIZED SHALLOTS

8 shallots, cut in half through the root, skins left on

2 tablespoons extra virgin olive oil, plus more for finishing

1 teaspoon fresh thyme leaves

Kosher salt and freshly ground black pepper, for seasoning

HELPFUL TOOLS

Sheet pan

Cast iron pan or heavy skillet

Meat thermometer

1 To make the steak: In a small bowl, combine the celery salt, sugar, black pepper, and cayenne. Rub the mixture all over the steak. Drizzle the steak with the olive oil and rub again to coat the steak. Wrap in plastic and let marinate in the refrigerator for at least 2 hours or up to overnight. Take the steak out of the fridge 1 hour before cooking.

2 To make the caramelized shallots: Preheat the oven to 400°F. Toss the shallots with the olive oil and thyme, then season with salt and pepper. Lay the shallots on a sheet pan, cut side down. Roast until the shallots are very tender, about 25 minutes. Set aside.

3 When you are ready to cook the steak, heat a large cast iron pan or heavy skillet over medium-high heat. Add the steak, and cook, turning once, until the internal temperature reads 125°F for medium rare, 5 to 6 minutes on each side. Take the steak out of the pan and let rest on a cutting board for 10 minutes.

4 While the pan is still hot, add the roasted shallots and heat through. Slice the steak against the grain and serve with the roasted shallots.

BRAISED SHORT RIBS
with Egg Noodles

Braising is a perfect choice for tougher pieces of meat like short ribs, since they need time to break down and create tender, fall-off-the bone goodness. During the cooking process, a magnificent broth develops, and the vegetables also take on a deep, rich flavor. When you're ready to serve, pair the beef with egg noodles. Their density holds up to the savory notes, and their curved shape holds some of the broth and pulled beef. *Serves 6*

4 tablespoons extra virgin olive oil, divided

6 thick bone-in center-cut short ribs, each about ¾ pound

Kosher salt and freshly ground black pepper

3 yellow onions, peeled and cut into eighths

4 medium carrots, cut into thick slices

2 large leeks, washed thoroughly and cut into thick slices

4 heads of garlic, halved crosswise

2 tablespoons coriander seeds

2 tablespoons black peppercorns

8 sprigs fresh rosemary

8 sprigs fresh thyme

2 fresh bay leaves

2 cups beef stock

2 cups red wine

12-ounce package egg noodles, cooked al dente

HELPFUL TOOLS

Dutch oven or lidded 8-quart heavy pot

Tongs

1 Preheat the oven to 325°F. Heat 2 tablespoons of the olive oil in a Dutch oven or heavy pot over high heat. Season the short ribs generously on all sides with salt and pepper. Add the meat to the pot and sear on all sides until browned, 5 to 10 minutes. Remove the short ribs from the pot with tongs and set aside.

2 Lower the heat to medium and add the remaining 2 tablespoons of olive oil to the pot. When the oil is hot but not smoking, add the onions, carrots, leeks, and 1 teaspoon salt. Cook, stirring occasionally, until the vegetables are soft, about 15 minutes. Add the garlic, coriander, peppercorns, rosemary, thyme, and bay leaves. Return the ribs to the pot, pour in the stock and wine to just cover the ribs, and bring to a simmer. Cover and transfer to the oven. Simmer the ribs, turning them every 30 minutes, until they are tender, about 3 hours.

3 Transfer the ribs to a platter. Let the braising liquid cool slightly until the grease floats to the top. Skim and discard the grease with a large spoon. Remove and discard the herb sprigs and bay leaves. Place the Dutch oven with degreased braising liquid over medium-high heat and bring it to a boil. Cook for 5 minutes, until the sauce has reduced and thickened. Plate the short ribs with a healthy spoonful of egg noodles, using the reduced braising liquid as a sauce.

THE BEST MESSY BURGER

Here's our Zakarian hamburger motto: When eating burgers, mess is best. They should be juicy, piled with delicious toppings, and deliver huge on beef taste. Also, do *not* kill your burger by overcooking it. The best taste comes from a high fat content in the beef, plus cooking it to medium-rare—or medium, max. If you cook it more than that, the meat will dry out. If you currently like a well-done burger, try little by little weaning off this preference by cooking the meat just a *tad* less each time.

The recipe forms four burgers, but if you prefer small burgers or sliders, simply divide the beef into smaller portions. *Serves 4*

FOR THE BURGER SAUCE

½ cup ketchup

½ cup mayonnaise

¼ cup finely chopped dill pickle

1 tablespoon prepared horseradish

1 teaspoon finely minced shallot

½ teaspoon kosher salt

¼ teaspoon freshly ground black pepper

FOR THE BURGERS

1½ pounds ground chuck (25 percent fat)

Kosher salt and freshly ground black pepper

1 teaspoon canola oil

8 slices sharp cheddar cheese

4 potato hamburger buns, with sesame seeds

Melted butter or extra virgin olive oil, for brushing

4 leaves Bibb or green-leaf lettuce

4 slices tomato

4 kosher dill pickle spears

HELPFUL TOOLS

4-inch ring cutter

Cast iron pan or griddle

1 To make the burger sauce: Combine the ketchup, mayonnaise, chopped pickle, horseradish, shallot, salt, and pepper. Set aside.

2 To make the burgers: Fit a small piece of plastic wrap inside a 4-inch ring cutter. Place about 6 ounces of ground chuck in the plastic and lightly press into the mold just to flatten a touch. Repeat with the remainder of the ground chuck. Generously season the patties with salt and pepper.

3 Heat the canola oil in a cast iron pan or griddle until it begins to smoke. Place the patties in the hot pan and sear on the first side, about 4 minutes. Flip and top each with two slices of cheese. Cook another 4 minutes on the other side for medium-rare. Remove the burgers from the pan and rest, about 10 minutes.

4 In the meantime, brush the cut sides of buns with butter or olive oil. Place cut side down in the hot pan and cook until lightly golden brown, about 1 to 2 minutes.

5 To assemble, place a patty on the bottom half of each bun and top with a lettuce leaf and a slice of tomato. Spread each bun top with some sauce, place on the patties, and serve with a pickle spear.

Burger Cooking Tips

- Season the patties generously with salt and pepper on both sides and edges.

- Patties should be cold when hitting griddle or grill.

- Let the patties rest for 5 to 10 minutes once they are done cooking. This prevents juices from running all over when you bite or cut them.

SIDES

SAUTÉED SPINACH & GARLIC

When we were little, under only *one* condition were we allowed to order pasta for dinner: if we had a first course of sautéed spinach. It was a deal we'd take every time, though now we eagerly eat spinach on our own. We've passed this tradition on to our little brother, George. Funny, he has nicknamed spinach "plants." Either way, plants + pasta = a great meal! *Serves 4*

2 tablespoons unsalted butter

2 tablespoons extra virgin olive oil

1 large shallot, chopped

2 small garlic cloves, minced

2 (10-ounce) bags fresh spinach, large stems removed

Kosher salt and freshly ground pepper

1   In a large sauté pan over medium heat, melt the butter in the olive oil. Add the shallot and garlic and sauté until softened, about 3 minutes.

2   Add half the spinach and stir until slightly wilted. Add the remaining spinach and continue to stir until the spinach is almost completely wilted and cooked down, about 2 minutes.

3   Remove from the heat and season to taste with salt and pepper. Serve.

Recipe pictured on page 97

TIP

Save any leftover spinach to use inside an omelet for breakfast the next day.

MEDITERRANEAN CAULIFLOWER

For some reason, cauliflower never seems to get the spotlight—but take our advice to start showing this vegetable some love. It's hearty, economical, and a good vehicle for stronger dressings, sauces, or spices. The cauliflower's versatility makes it a well-suited side dish for a variety of meals, so we have a habit of always keeping a head in the fridge. *Serves 4*

1 large head of cauliflower, core removed, cut into medium florets

3 tablespoons extra virgin olive oil, divided

2 tablespoons sesame seeds

1 teaspoon kosher salt

3 tablespoons tahini

2 tablespoons freshly squeezed lemon juice

1 tablespoon water

1 small garlic clove, minced

¼ teaspoon freshly ground black pepper

6 fresh mint leaves, torn into small pieces, for garnish

Large flake sea salt, for finishing

HELPFUL TOOLS

Sheet pan

1   Preheat the oven to 425°F. Place the cauliflower florets in a large mixing bowl and toss with 2 tablespoons of the olive oil, the sesame seeds, and salt. Place the cauliflower in a single layer on a sheet pan, then place the pan in the oven. Roast, stirring occasionally, until the cauliflower is caramelized, about 25 minutes.

2   Meanwhile, in a small mixing bowl, whisk together the remaining 1 tablespoon olive oil, the tahini, lemon juice, water, garlic, and pepper.

3   Transfer the roasted cauliflower to a serving bowl, add the tahini sauce, and toss. Garnish with the mint and season with sea salt. Serve.

Recipe pictured on page 97

Honey
Carrots
PAGE 98

Sautéed
Spinach &
Garlic
PAGE 94

Mediterranean
Cauliflower
PAGE 95

HONEY CARROTS

Orange juice and carrots are a match made in kitchen heaven. As they cook together with honey, bright, citrusy notes and natural sweetness develop in the glaze, giving you an easy yet "foodie" upgrade to steaming this common root vegetable. *Serves 4*

1 tablespoon kosher salt, plus more for seasoning

1 pound baby carrots, peeled

3 tablespoons unsalted butter

3 tablespoons honey

1 tablespoon freshly squeezed orange juice

Freshly ground black pepper

1 Fill a medium saucepan with water, add the salt, and bring to a boil. Add the carrots and cook until fork-tender, 6 to 8 minutes. Remove from the heat and drain.

2 In a large sauté pan, melt the butter over medium heat. Add the honey and orange juice, then stir to combine. Add the carrots and cook, stirring occasionally, until a glaze forms on the carrots, about 5 minutes.

3 Remove from the heat and spoon the carrots into a serving dish. Season with additional salt and pepper and serve.

For an added crunch, garnish with ¼ cup of toasted chopped walnuts before serving.

Recipe pictured on page 96

MUSTARD POTATOES
with Apples & Herbs

This is the perfect item to serve with roast chicken, and it's also quite versatile. It can be served hot from the stovetop, brought along for a meal outdoors to enjoy at room temperature, or even reheated at a potluck dinner. This crowd-pleasing side dish is an A+ for sure. **Serves 4**

2 pounds fingerling potatoes

2 tablespoons kosher salt, plus more for seasoning

¼ cup extra virgin olive oil

2 cloves garlic, peeled

4 sprigs fresh thyme

1 tart apple, peeled, cored, and cut into 8 wedges

1 tablespoon finely chopped fresh parsley

1 tablespoon finely minced chives

1 tablespoon finely chopped fresh tarragon

Grated zest and juice of 1 lemon

2 tablespoons grainy mustard

Freshly ground black pepper

1 In a medium saucepan, cover the potatoes with cold water. Add the salt and bring the water to a slow boil over high heat. Reduce the heat and simmer the potatoes for 6 to 8 minutes, until tender. Drain the potatoes and cool under running water. Once cool, slice each potato lengthwise in half.

2 Heat the olive oil in a large sauté pan over medium heat. Add the garlic cloves and thyme and cook until the garlic turns golden brown. Remove the pan from heat and carefully scoop out the garlic and thyme, then throw both away.

3 Return the pan to the heat and add the potatoes, cut side down. Add the apple wedges and cook until both are golden brown. Add the parsley, chives, tarragon, lemon zest, and mustard. Continue to cook for 1 minute.

4 Transfer the potatoes to a serving bowl and toss with the lemon juice. Season to taste with salt and pepper, then serve.

Recipe pictured on page 100

Fragrant
Rice Pilaf
PAGE 101

Mustard Potatoes
with Apples & Herbs
PAGE 99

FRAGRANT RICE PILAF

We really, really like to eat rice, and being Lebanese, rice pilaf ranks high on our list of favorite sides. With this recipe, we've switched up the traditional version by adding a few extra ingredients. The enchanting smell of the dish comes from taking the time at the beginning of the recipe to toast the spices. *Serves 4*

4 tablespoons unsalted butter

1 medium onion, diced

¾ teaspoon ground cumin

¾ teaspoon turmeric

¾ teaspoon ground cinnamon

2 cloves garlic, minced

2 cups basmati rice

3 cups water

2 teaspoons kosher salt

½ teaspoon freshly ground black pepper

½ cup dried raisins

½ cup sliced almonds, toasted

1   Melt the butter in a medium pot over medium heat. Add the onion and cook until softened, about 4 minutes. Add the cumin, turmeric, cinnamon, and garlic and cook until fragrant, about 1 minute.

2   Add the rice and cook, stirring constantly, for about 3 minutes. Add the water, salt, and pepper and bring to a boil. Reduce the heat to low, cover, and simmer until all the liquid is absorbed, about 18 minutes. Remove from the heat.

3   Sprinkle the raisins and almonds over the rice, fluff with a fork, and serve.

STEAMED PONZU BROCCOLI

Ponzu is a sunnier, happier soy sauce that is made from soy and yuzu, a Japanese citrus that's more floral and less acidic than lemon. The actual fruit can be difficult to get your hands on, but a bottle of ponzu should be available at most large grocers and easily available online. Here, we make our own version. Used with broccoli, ponzu gives new life to the traditional dinner-table staple. *Serves 4*

½ cup reduced-sodium soy sauce or tamari (gluten-free soy sauce)

¼ cup orange juice

2 tablespoons fresh lime juice (from 1 large lime)

1 tablespoon mirin

1 tablespoon water

⅛ teaspoon crushed red pepper flakes

4 cups broccoli florets

Fried shallots, for garnish

HELPFUL TOOLS
Steamer basket

1 To make the ponzu: In a medium mixing bowl, whisk together the soy sauce, orange juice, lime juice, mirin, water, and pepper flakes. Set aside.

2 Bring 1 inch of water to a boil in a medium saucepan with a steamer basket. Place the broccoli in the steamer, cover the pot, and reduce the heat to a simmer. Steam the broccoli for 5 to 6 minutes, until you can easily pierce the florets with a fork.

3 Place the steamed broccoli on a serving platter and drizzle with the ponzu. (Unused sauce will keep in the refrigerator for up to 1 week.) Garnish with fried shallots and serve.

RATATOUILLE

The idea of ratatouille was ingrained in us before we even tasted it. From a very young age, we repeatedly watched a movie about a "tiny chef" who lands himself in Paris, where he captivates a food critic with his mastery of a simple peasant dish. The movie, named after this dish, shows ratatouille two ways: 1) a plated version with perfect layers of vegetables, and 2) a homespun version served in a bowl. In real life, the aroma is the same coming from either version, and for many people this smell brings happy memories of their mother's comfort cooking. Have fun with this, and once you've mastered the seasoning, experiment with your own style of slicing, dicing, and plating. You can make this for many decades to come. It's a trusted classic. **Serves 4**

6 tablespoons extra virgin olive oil, divided, plus more for serving

1½ pounds purple eggplant (about 1 large), cut into large dice

Kosher salt and freshly ground black pepper

¾ zucchini, cut into large dice

¾ yellow summer squash, cut into large dice

1 medium yellow onion, diced

1 large red bell pepper, cut into large dice

2 cloves garlic, minced

2 sprigs fresh thyme

1 bay leaf

1 pound tomatoes (3 to 4 medium), cut into large dice

¼ cup loosely packed fresh basil leaves, thinly sliced

HELPFUL TOOLS

Dutch oven or large pot

1   In a Dutch oven or large pot, heat 2 tablespoons of the olive oil over medium heat. Add the eggplant, season generously with salt and pepper, and cook, stirring occasionally, until browned in spots, about 2 minutes. Transfer to a large bowl.

2   In the same pot, heat 2 tablespoons olive oil over medium heat. Add the zucchini and yellow squash, season generously with salt and pepper, and cook, stirring occasionally, until browned in spots, about 2 minutes. Transfer to the bowl with the eggplant.

3   Return the pot to medium heat and add the remaining 2 tablespoons olive oil. Add the onion and red bell pepper, season with salt and pepper, and cook, stirring occasionally, until softened and just beginning to brown, 6 to 8 minutes.

4   Stir the garlic, thyme, bay leaf, and tomatoes into the pot. Stir in the reserved eggplant, zucchini, and yellow squash. Bring to a simmer, then turn down the heat to low and simmer, stirring occasionally, for about 1 hour.

5   Fish out the bay leaf and thyme sprigs and discard. Taste the ratatouille and season with salt and pepper. Stir in the fresh basil and serve with a drizzle of olive oil.

DESSERT

TROPICAL PINEAPPLE & LIME

We usually enjoy this on a weeknight after dinner, when we're in the mood for dessert and Mom says treats and sugar are done for the day. Experiment with the way you cut the pineapple, like making long spears, or cutting very thin slices to lay out flat on a plate like carpaccio. *Serves 6 to 8*

1 ripe pineapple, peeled, cored, and sliced into ¼-inch-thick pieces

1 lime

¼ teaspoon kosher salt

Lime wedges and mint leaves, for garnish

HELPFUL TOOLS

Microplane zester

1 Arrange the pineapple wedges on a platter and grate the zest of the lime directly over the fruit. Cut the lime in half and squeeze juice over the top, then sprinkle with salt.

2 Garnish with lime wedges and mint leaves and serve.

To pick a ripe pineapple, give it a squeeze: You should feel a slight give in the flesh when you press against the sides, as well as a fragrant aroma coming from the bottom of the core.

DECADENT BROWNIE TART

If you want to really wow your guests with a chocolate crowd-pleaser, make this tart! Because of the deep, robust flavors of the coffee and chocolate in the tart, it's important to have a creamy partner when plating. Vanilla bean ice cream is always a winner, but whipped cream or crème fraîche are worthy substitutes. *Serves 8*

1 cup hazelnuts, lightly toasted

1½ cups sugar, divided

½ cup plus 1 tablespoon unsweetened cocoa powder

½ teaspoon kosher salt

16 tablespoons (2 sticks) unsalted butter

1 cup bittersweet chocolate chips

3 large eggs

1 tablespoon instant coffee dissolved in 1 tablespoon hot water

Vanilla bean ice cream, for serving

HELPFUL TOOLS

9-inch springform pan with removable sides, or fluted 9-inch tart pan with removable bottom

Nonstick cooking spray

Food processor

Silicone spatula

Stand mixer with whisk attachment

1 Preheat the oven to 325°F. Spray a 9-inch springform pan with nonstick cooking spray. In a food processor, combine the hazelnuts, ¼ cup of the sugar, the cocoa, and salt and pulse until finely ground. Set aside.

2 In a medium saucepan, melt the butter over medium heat, then cook, swirling the pan occasionally, until nutty-smelling and deep golden in color, about 5 minutes. Remove from the heat and add the chocolate chips. Let stand until melted, about 2 minutes. Whisk the butter and chocolate until smooth, scraping up any browned butter solids from the bottom of the pan with a silicone spatula. Let cool slightly.

3 In the bowl of a stand mixer fitted with the whisk attachment, beat the remaining 1¼ cups sugar with the eggs and the coffee mixture on medium speed for about 5 minutes. With the mixer on low, add the chocolate-butter mixture, followed by the cocoa-hazelnut mixture.

4 With the spatula, scrape the batter into the prepared pan. Bake the tart for about 35 minutes, or until the top is glossy and a toothpick inserted in the center comes out with a few moist crumbs attached. Let the brownie tart cool on a rack for 30 minutes in the pan. Remove from the pan, cut into wedges, and top with ice cream to serve.

CLASSIC FRENCH STRAWBERRY SOUFFLÉS

In its simplest form, a soufflé is beaten egg whites that rise in a hot oven. Many varieties of soufflés (such as chocolate, cheese, and Grand Marnier) have graced the menus of French restaurants around the world, but strawberry is the best one to learn first. We are lucky enough to have a dad who encouraged us to try making our own soufflés, and honestly, if he hadn't, we probably would have never tried. So to pay it forward, consider this a gentle push to give it a try yourself. It's not as hard as everyone says! *Serves 6*

3 tablespoons unsalted butter, softened, for brushing ramekins

½ cup granulated sugar, plus more for coating ramekins

½ cup strawberries, hulled and sliced; plus more for topping

1 teaspoon vanilla paste or vanilla extract

8 large egg whites, at room temperature

½ teaspoon cream of tartar

½ cup powdered sugar, plus more for dusting

HELPFUL TOOLS

Pastry brush, optional

8-ounce soufflé ramekins

Sheet pan

Blender

Silicone spatula

Stand mixer with whisk attachment

1 Position a rack in the lower part of the oven, leaving plenty of room above for the soufflés to rise. Preheat the oven to 375°F.

2 With a pastry brush or your hands, generously butter the insides of six soufflé ramekins. Add some granulated sugar to each ramekin, and swirl and turn the ramekin to evenly coat the interior with sugar. Place the ramekins on a sheet pan.

3 In a blender, puree the strawberries with the ½ cup granulated sugar. Add the vanilla. Process until very smooth, then scrape the puree into a bowl with a silicone spatula.

4 In the bowl of a stand mixer fitted with a whisk attachment, begin to whip the egg whites and cream of tartar on medium speed. Gradually add the powdered sugar. Continue to whip until the meringue is very firm, stands up straight when the whisk is lifted, and the appearance is shiny. This could take 5 to 10 minutes or longer, depending on the temperature of the egg whites.

5 Remove the bowl from the mixer. With the spatula, gently fold half of the strawberry puree into the egg whites. (Reserve the other half for serving.) Divide the strawberry meringue among the prepared ramekins; they should be slightly overfilled. Lightly tap each ramekin against the counter. Decoratively place strawberry slices on top of the soufflés.

6 Place the sheet pan in the oven and bake the soufflés for about 15 minutes, or until very puffy and set. Dust with powdered sugar and serve *immediately* with the remaining strawberry puree.

Recipe Continues

- Room temperature egg whites whip best. Separate the eggs an hour before starting and leave the whites out on the counter to warm up.

- If you don't have a stand mixer, you can use a handheld mixer.

- In a stand mixer, egg whites could take approximately 10 minutes to beat.

- Butter is ideal, but nonstick cooking spray may be substituted to grease the ramekins for a dairy-free option.

- Once ramekins are filled with the meringue, try not to shake or move them too much.

- Leave the oven shut once the soufflés go in.

- Try the recipe again if they do not rise on the first try.

HEARTWARMING APPLE CRUMBLE

Well-suited for a group, apple crumble can lovingly end a meal in a way that no other dessert can. To save time, make the filling and topping ahead and store separately in the fridge for up to 1 day. Or you can completely assemble and bake the crumble, then freeze to serve at a later date. **Serves 6 to 8**

FOR THE STREUSEL TOPPING

1 cup all-purpose flour

¾ cup rolled oats

½ cup packed light brown sugar

½ teaspoon ground cinnamon

¼ teaspoon salt

8 tablespoons (1 stick) unsalted butter, chilled and cut into small pieces

FOR THE APPLE FILLING

Unsalted butter, at room temperature, for greasing the pan

6 firm tart apples (such as Cortland), peeled, cored, and cut into ¼-inch-thick slices

Juice of 1 lemon

½ cup granulated sugar

2 tablespoons all-purpose flour

¼ teaspoon ground cinnamon

HELPFUL TOOLS

2-quart baking dish

1 To make the streusel topping: In a medium bowl, combine the flour, oats, brown sugar, cinnamon, and salt. With your fingers, rub the butter into the flour mixture until you no longer see butter chunks and the streusel clumps together easily.

2 To make the apple filling: Preheat the oven to 350°F. Lightly coat the inside of a 2-quart baking dish with butter. In a large mixing bowl, toss together the apple slices, lemon juice, granulated sugar, flour, and cinnamon. Pour the filling into the prepared baking dish and spread in an even layer. Top with the streusel topping, pinching it together to form larger clumps.

3 Place the dish in the oven and bake the crumble for about 1 hour, or until the fruit is bubbling and the topping is golden brown. Let cool for about 30 minutes and serve warm.

SUMMER PANNA COTTA
with Peaches

Panna cotta is a chilled Italian dessert made from yogurt, and we suggest you think of it as a blank canvas. Once it's set, you can top it with a variety of items. Here we have chosen honey and peaches.
Serves 6

1 envelope (¼ ounce or 1 tablespoon) unflavored gelatin powder

¼ cup cold water

1½ cups heavy cream, divided

⅓ cup granulated sugar

⅛ teaspoon kosher salt

2 cups plain whole-milk Greek yogurt

1 teaspoon vanilla extract

1 ripe peach, pitted and cut into thin slices

Fresh honeycomb or honey, for garnish

1 Sprinkle the gelatin over the cold water in a small bowl and let soften for about 5 minutes. This is called blooming the gelatin.

2 In a small saucepan, gently heat 1 cup of the cream with the sugar and salt, stirring until the sugar has dissolved. Remove from the heat and stir in the bloomed gelatin and its water until the gelatin is fully dissolved.

3 Whisk together the yogurt and remaining ½ cup cream in a bowl until combined. Whisk in the gelatin mixture and vanilla and divide among six serving dishes. Cover and refrigerate until set and firm, at least 2 hours, or up to overnight.

4 When ready to serve, top each panna cotta with peach slices and a small piece of fresh honeycomb or a drizzle of honey.

 In the winter, try topping this dessert with jam, pomegranates, or pears.

PASTEL MERINGUE CLOUDS

These are basically sweet dreamy clouds that look as good as they taste! We like to make large ones with beautiful colors for a big impact, or teeny-tiny ones to use as a topping for ice cream sundaes. Have fun with these, and consider preparing a double batch while you are at it, as they store well and you'll be happy to have more for later. *Makes 12 large meringues*

5 large egg whites, at room temperature

½ teaspoon cream of tartar

3 cups granulated sugar

2 tablespoons vanilla extract

Gel paste food coloring, your choice of pastel hues

HELPFUL TOOLS

Sheet pans

Parchment paper or Silpat baking mats

Stand mixer with whisk attachment

Silicone spatula

1 Preheat the oven to 225°F. Line two sheet pans with parchment paper or Silpat mats.

2 Place the egg whites and cream of tartar in the bowl of a stand mixer fitted with the whisk attachment. Beat on medium speed until the whites begin to froth. Then, while the mixer is still going, begin gradually adding the sugar. Once all the sugar has been added, add the vanilla and continue beating until stiff, glossy peaks form. This could take as long as 10 minutes, depending on temperature of the egg whites when you start.

3 Divide the meringue between two bowls. Add 1 small drop of gel paste food coloring to each bowl and carefully, with a silicone spatula, fold until fully incorporated.

4 With a large spoon, drop six large dollops of meringue onto each sheet pan. Bake for 2 hours, or until the meringues are cooked through, firm on the outside, but still chewy on the inside. If yours are not done, you can turn off the heat and leave them in the oven for longer. Store meringues in an airtight container to keep fresh for up to 2 weeks.

Letting the merengues cool in the oven overnight is a pro move that can help prevent cracks from appearing on the tops.

MAGIC CHOCOLATE MOUSSE

This mousse is truly chocolate heaven, minus the refined sugar and dairy. Sounds impossible, right? Here's how the magic works: The star ingredient, overripe bananas, sweetens the mousse because as bananas ripen, the natural sugars inside continue to increase. Avocado creates the creamy, buttery texture, and cocoa powder ties it all together in an amazingly crave-worthy bow. *Serves 2 to 4*

1 ripe avocado, pitted, peeled, and diced

2 large ripe to overripe bananas, peeled and cut into large pieces

5 tablespoons unsweetened cocoa powder

2 tablespoons pure maple syrup

Generous pinch of salt

Fresh raspberries, for garnish

Cocoa nibs, for garnish

HELPFUL TOOLS

Blender or food processor (mini or regular)

1   Combine the avocado, bananas, cocoa, maple syrup, and salt in a blender or food processor. Process on high speed for 1 minute, or until smooth and creamy.

2   Transfer the mousse to a bowl or glass jars and refrigerate for 1 hour before serving. Top with fresh raspberries (or other fruit), and a sprinkle of cocoa nibs, then serve.

 Mousse can be served immediately if necessary.

VANILLA BEAN SHORTBREAD

If you can master the shortbread method, you'll suddenly have so many fantastic cookie options at your fingertips. We start with simple vanilla for this recipe, and from there we suggest chocolate chip and pistachio. The possibilities—and shapes—are endless! *Makes 2 dozen cookies*

2 cups all-purpose flour

½ teaspoon kosher salt

16 tablespoons (2 sticks) unsalted butter, at room temperature

½ cup powdered sugar

1 teaspoon vanilla extract

½ of a vanilla bean, halved lengthwise and seeds scraped out

HELPFUL TOOLS

Stand mixer with paddle attachment

Silicone spatula

Rolling pin

Sheet pans

Parchment paper or Silpat mats

Cookie cutter; we like a 3-inch round or oval cutter for this recipe

1   In a small bowl, sift together the flour and salt. In a mixer fitted with the paddle attachment, mix the butter and sugar together on high speed until light and fluffy. With a silicone spatula, scrape down sides of the bowl and add the vanilla extract and vanilla bean seeds. Mix again until combined. Add the flour mixture and carefully mix until just combined.

2   Remove the dough from the bowl and wrap in plastic wrap. Using a rolling pin, flatten into an 8-inch disc. Refrigerate until firm, about 1 hour.

3   Preheat the oven to 325°F. Line two sheet pans with parchment paper or Silpat mats. Remove the dough from the refrigerator. On a well-floured surface with a floured rolling pin, roll out the dough to a ¼-inch thickness. Use plenty of flour when rolling so the dough doesn't stick. Cut into desired shapes using a cookie cutter and place on a sheet pan about an inch apart. Wrap the scraps in plastic wrap and place back into the fridge. After baking the first batch, you can reroll scraps and cut out more cookies to bake.

4   Bake the cookies for 12 to 15 minutes, until firm and very light golden brown around the edges. Remove from the oven and cool completely on a cooling rack.

Variations

CHOCOLATE CHIP SHORTBREAD: Add 1 cup bittersweet chocolate chips after adding the flour mixture and lightly mix to distribute evenly.

PISTACHIO SHORTBREAD: Add 1 cup chopped pistachio pieces after adding the flour mixture and lightly mix to distribute evenly.

Place the scraped vanilla pod in an airtight container with 1 cup granulated sugar, then shake. Keep this homemade vanilla sugar for use in future baking or warm drinks.

WHIPPED CREAM FOREVER

Everyone loves whipped cream, and knowing how to quickly make it adds so much versatility to your desserts and warm drinks. Plus, you won't have to buy it anymore. It's a pretty simple method, so we suggest memorizing it *forever!* ***Makes 6 servings***

1 cup cold heavy cream or whipping cream, straight from the refrigerator

2 tablespoons powdered sugar

1 teaspoon vanilla extract

HELPFUL TOOLS

Stand mixer with whisk attachment or handheld mixer

In the bowl of a stand mixer fitted with a whisk attachment or a medium mixing bowl with a handheld mixer, combine the cream, sugar, and vanilla. Beat on medium speed until medium peaks form, about 4 minutes. Use immediately or cover and store in the refrigerator for up to 3 days.

Variations

CHOCOLATE WHIPPED CREAM: Lightly mix 1 tablespoon cocoa powder into the powdered sugar before adding to the cream.

ALMOND WHIPPED CREAM: Add ½ teaspoon almond extract along with the vanilla extract.

The cream should be as cold as possible. Chill the bowl and whisk attachments in the freezer for about 10 minutes before whipping.

SNACKS

OLIVE OIL GRANOLA BARS

We used to buy a lot of packaged snacks but realized we could make *much* more delicious snacks on our own. During our learning process, we decided to tackle granola bars first, because when they are made with the right ingredients, they have a hearty helping of protein, will keep you filled, and are easy to transport. **Makes 12 bars**

2 cups rolled oats, divided

½ cup packed light brown sugar

¾ cup dried cherries or cranberries

½ cup unsalted whole roasted almonds

½ cup pumpkin seeds

½ cup sunflower seeds

½ teaspoon ground cinnamon

½ teaspoon kosher salt

½ cup smooth peanut butter or other nut butter

½ cup extra virgin olive oil

½ cup maple syrup

HELPFUL TOOLS

8x8-inch baking dish

Parchment paper

Nonstick cooking spray

Food processor

1   Preheat the oven to 350°F. Line an 8x8-inch baking dish with parchment paper, then lightly grease the paper with nonstick cooking spray. In a food processor, blend ⅓ cup of the oats until finely ground.

2   In a large mixing bowl, stir together the ground oats, remaining 1⅔ cups oats, brown sugar, dried cherries, almonds, pumpkin seeds, sunflower seeds, cinnamon, and salt. In a small bowl, whisk together the peanut butter, olive oil, and maple syrup. Add the wet mixture to the dry mixture and stir until thoroughly combined.

3   Spread the mixture evenly in the prepared pan. Bake for about 30 minutes, or until the top starts to brown and the edges are golden. Let cool in pan completely, then remove and cut into 12 bars. Bars can stay in an airtight container for up to a week.

 If you're finding the bars hard to cut, ask an adult for help. Their height will lend helpful leverage.

POWER-UP SNACK BALLS

Boom! These pack a powerful punch. They're fun to make and healthy to eat. If you have some friends over, stack them high, or if you are on the move, bring a few along. *Makes 18 snack balls*

1¼ cups rolled oats

½ cup almond butter

⅓ cup honey

1 tablespoon chia seeds

1 tablespoon flax seeds

1 teaspoon vanilla extract

¼ teaspoon kosher salt

HELPFUL TOOLS

Sheet pan

1   Combine all ingredients in a large bowl and use your hands to thoroughly mix together. Cover with plastic wrap and refrigerate for 30 minutes.

2   Using a small cookie scoop or spoon, scoop 1-inch balls of the mixture onto a sheet pan. Roll each between your hands and place back on the pan. Store in the refrigerator in an airtight container for up to 2 weeks.

Variations

WHITE CHOCOLATE CRANBERRY BALLS: Add ¼ cup dried cranberries and ¼ cup white chocolate chips to the base recipe.

DOUBLE CHOCOLATE BALLS: Add ½ cup mini chocolate chips and 2 tablespoons cocoa powder to the base recipe.

OATMEAL RAISIN BALLS: Add ½ cup raisins and ¼ teaspoon ground cinnamon to the base recipe.

Almond butters vary in consistency—some loose, others more firm—which can cause a variation when using this ingredient. If your snack ball mixture needs more almond butter to help ingredients stick together, gradually add in up to ¼ cup more.

CREAMY HUMMUS
with Crudités

We always keep hummus in the fridge to snack on. Admittedly, we default at times by purchasing the premade kind at the grocery store (eek! shame!), but when we do make it at home, we're quickly reminded of just how rewarding it is to make ourselves. *Serves 6 or more*

1 (15-ounce) can chickpeas

1 large clove garlic, roughly chopped

⅓ cup fresh lemon juice (from 2 lemons), plus more for seasoning

½ teaspoon kosher salt, plus more for seasoning

½ cup tahini

2 tablespoons ice water, plus more if necessary

½ teaspoon ground cumin

2 tablespoons extra virgin olive oil, plus more for drizzling

Chopped fresh parsley, for garnish

Freshly cut assortment of crudités (carrots, radishes, snow peas, and other in-season vegetables)

HELPFUL TOOLS

Food processor

Silicone spatula

1   Drain the chickpeas in a strainer and run cool water over them to rinse.

2   In a food processor, puree the garlic, lemon juice, and salt until the garlic is finely chopped. Add the tahini and blend until the mixture is thick and creamy. Scrape with a silicone spatula and blend a few seconds more. While running the food processor, drizzle in the ice water. Scrape down the food processor and blend until the mixture is very smooth, pale, and creamy.

3   Add the chickpeas and cumin to the food processor. While blending, drizzle in the olive oil, then continue to blend, scraping down the sides of the food processor as necessary, until the mixture is super smooth, about 2 minutes. Add more ice water by the tablespoon if needed to achieve a super creamy texture. Taste and season with additional salt and lemon juice.

4   Scrape the hummus into a serving bowl. Garnish with a healthy drizzle of olive oil and parsley. Serve immediately with crudités on the side.

**Creamy Hummus
with Crudités**
PAGE 134

**Everything
Cheddar Crackers**
PAGE 136

EVERYTHING CHEDDAR CRACKERS

The dough for these crackers freezes well, so you can make multiple batches and pull them out of the freezer when you want to make more snacks. For an easy variation, swap out the everything topping for your favorite dried herbs. ***Makes about 60 crackers***

EVERYTHING TOPPING

2 tablespoons dried onion

1 tablespoon dried minced garlic

1 tablespoon black sesame seeds

1 tablespoon sesame seeds

1 tablespoon poppy seeds

1 tablespoon kosher salt

CRACKER DOUGH

10 ounces sharp cheddar cheese, shredded

1½ cups all-purpose flour

8 tablespoons (1 stick) unsalted butter, cut into small cubes

¼ teaspoon cayenne pepper

3 tablespoons half-and-half

1 large egg

2 teaspoons water

HELPFUL TOOLS

Food processor

Sheet pan

Parchment paper

1½-inch square or round fluted cookie cutter

Rolling pin, if needed

1 To make the everything topping: In a small bowl, stir together all the ingredients and set aside.

2 To make the cracker dough: In a food processor, combine the cheese, flour, butter, and cayenne pepper and pulse until the mixture resembles coarse crumbs. Add the half-and-half and blend until the mixture forms a ball. Divide into two balls, flatten slightly, and wrap in plastic wrap. Refrigerate for 15 minutes.

3 Preheat the oven to 350°F. Line a sheet pan with parchment paper and set aside. On a floured surface, roll out one piece of dough to ¼-inch thickness. With a 1½-inch square or round fluted cookie cutter, cut out squares or rounds and place on the prepared sheet about 1 inch apart.

4 Whisk together the egg and water. Brush the tops of the crackers with the egg wash, then sprinkle with everything topping. If the topping doesn't stick, place another sheet of parchment on top of the crackers and lightly roll the paper with a rolling pin to press in the seasoning.

5 Bake for 15 to 18 minutes, until golden brown. Repeat with remaining dough. Baked crackers can be stored in a sealed container for up to 1 week.

Recipe pictured on page 135

HOMEMADE POTATO CHIPS

This is another item that we often buy from the store, but when we make it ourselves, we always think, "Why do we ever buy chips!?" Seriously, homemade is one-thousand times better. These should definitely be made with an adult's help, as extra precaution is a must with hot oil. Also, consider doubling the recipe and storing extra chips in an airtight container for up to a week. You'll be glad you did. *Serves 4*

2 large russet potatoes (unpeeled)

Up to 2 quarts canola oil, for frying

Kosher salt, for sprinkling

HELPFUL TOOLS

Mandoline

Large stockpot and deep-fry thermometer, or a deep fryer

Spider or slotted spoon

Sheet pan with rack

1 Using a mandoline set at 1/16th inch or a sharp knife, slice the potatoes. Put all the slices in a big bowl of cold water and let sit for at least 20 minutes.

2 Meanwhile, fill a large stockpot halfway with canola oil or a countertop deep fryer to the fill line. Heat the oil to 375°F. Drain as much water as you can from the potato slices, then use paper towels to absorb any additional water on the surface.

3 Working in batches, place the potato slices in the hot oil. Using a slotted spoon or a spider, move the potato chips around so that the slices do not stick to each other and are completely submerged under the oil. Fry until golden brown and the chip slices stop bubbling. Remove to a sheet pan with a rack so the grease can drain. While the chips are hot, immediately season generously with salt.

Variations

ROSEMARY POTATO CHIPS:
Finely chop 1 tablespoon fresh rosemary and combine with 1 tablespoon kosher salt. Season the potato chips with the rosemary salt to your liking immediately after frying. Add more salt to taste if necessary.

SALT AND VINEGAR POTATO CHIPS:
Sprinkle 2 tablespoons malt vinegar onto chips after frying and season with salt as directed.

Homemade
Potato Chips
PAGE 137

SEA SALT KALE CHIPS

We're big-time fans of these kale chips as an alternative to potato chips. They taste amazing, partly because massaging the oil into the leaves means nice, even crisping. Definitely consider doubling the recipe, because every time we make it, all the chips end up gone before we can store them! *Serves 4*

5 to 6 hearty green kale leaves, washed and dried

3 tablespoons extra virgin olive oil

1 teaspoon sea salt, plus more for seasoning

HELPFUL TOOLS

2 sheet pans

Parchment paper

1   Preheat the oven to 325°F. Cut or rip out the ribs from each kale leaf. Cut or rip the leaves into 1-inch pieces and place in a bowl. Drizzle the olive oil over all, then massage the oil into all the leaves with your hands. Toss with the salt.

2   Line two sheet pans with parchment paper. Divide the kale leaves between the two pans and bake until crispy, but not brown, 15 to 20 minutes. Season with additional salt if necessary, then serve.

SOFT BAKED PRETZELS & PURPLE MUSTARD

Making pretzels is a more advanced multistep recipe involving shaping the dough, boiling it, and then finally baking that may take some practice. Despite the extra work, there is the high reward of eating a warm pretzel straight from the oven, especially when it's one that you made yourself! However, you can easily whip up the purple mustard included here anytime, to use as a dipping sauce for a variety of things. *Makes 6 pretzels and dipping sauce*

FOR THE PURPLE MUSTARD

½ cup brown or Dijon mustard

2 teaspoons beetroot powder

FOR THE PRETZELS

4 cups all-purpose flour

1 tablespoon sugar

2 teaspoons kosher salt

½ teaspoon active dry yeast

1½ cups warm water (105°F)

5 tablespoons unsalted butter, melted, plus more for brushing

8 cups water

¼ cup baking soda

Coarse pretzel salt, for finishing

HELPFUL TOOLS

Stand mixer with dough hook

Digital thermometer (for taking the temperature of the water)

Parchment paper

Sheet pans

Tongs

1 To make the purple mustard: In a small bowl, whisk together the mustard and beetroot powder, then set aside.

2 To make the pretzels: In the bowl of a stand mixer fitted with a dough hook, combine the flour, sugar, salt, and yeast. With the mixer running on low, slowly add the warm water. Mix briefly to incorporate. Add the melted butter, then mix on medium speed for about 5 minutes. The dough will form a loose ball and pull away from the sides of the bowl. Transfer the dough to an oiled bowl, cover with plastic wrap, and let rise at room temperature for about 1 hour, or until it has doubled in size.

3 Preheat the oven to 400°F. Turn the dough onto a floured work surface and divide into six equal portions. For each pretzel, roll one portion of dough into a long, slender log about 10 to 12 inches long. Shape the dough into a horseshoe shape, with the ends of the "U" pointed up. Overlap the ends, leaving approximately 2-inch "tails," then flip the overlapping ends down, so that they meet the bottom of the rounded part. Place on a parchment-lined sheet pan and repeat with the remaining dough.

4 Bring the water and baking soda to a boil in a large stockpot. Once the baking soda is dissolved, turn the heat to low. Working in batches, drop the pretzels into the water and poach for 10 to 15 seconds. Flip with tongs, then continue poaching on the second side for 10 to 15 seconds. Remove the pretzels with a slotted spoon and place on another sheet pan lined with parchment paper.

5 Coat each pretzel generously with pretzel salt. Bake for 10 to 12 minutes, until golden brown. Brush the pretzels with melted butter and serve with the purple mustard.

TOMATO & HERB FOCACCIA

When focaccia, Italian flatbread, comes out of the oven, it'll fill your kitchen with an incredible aroma, thanks to the herbs and olive oil, making it a great choice if you want to put a smile on the face of anyone nearby. It's also nice to make when you've invited friends over who may not all know each other. The smell will pull them right into the kitchen as they arrive, getting them eating and sharing quickly. *Serves 6 to 8*

1 packet (2¼ teaspoons) active dry yeast

1¾ cups warm water

5½ cups all-purpose flour, plus more if needed

1 tablespoon granulated sugar

1 tablespoon plus 1 teaspoon kosher salt, divided

¾ cup extra virgin olive oil, divided, plus more for oiling the bowl and drizzling on top

1 tablespoon chopped fresh rosemary

1 cup cherry tomatoes, cut in half

HELPFUL TOOLS

Stand mixer with hook attachment

Large sheet pan

Cooling rack

Pizza cutting wheel

1   In a small bowl, sprinkle the yeast over the warm water and stir to dissolve. Let bloom until activated, about 5 minutes.

2   In the bowl of a stand mixer fitted with the hook attachment, combine the yeast mixture, flour, sugar, 1 tablespoon of the salt, and ½ cup of the olive oil. Start on low speed and mix until the ingredients are combined. Increase the mixer to medium and continue to mix until the dough comes together in a sticky ball, adding more flour if necessary.

3   Transfer the dough to an oiled bowl. Cover with plastic wrap and let sit in a warm spot until almost doubled in size, about 1 hour.

4   Pour the remaining ¼ cup olive oil evenly onto a sheet pan. Place the dough on the sheet pan, flipping over once to coat with oil. Use fingers to stretch and spread it into the corners and then create dimples all over the top. Scatter the rosemary over the dough and season with the remaining 1 teaspoon salt. Press the tomatoes, cut side up, randomly into dough. Let the dough sit and rise for 30 minutes on the countertop.

5   Preheat the oven to 375°F. Place the sheet pan in the oven and bake the focaccia for 25 to 30 minutes, until golden brown. Remove the pan from the oven and place on a cooling rack. Let cool slightly, then cut into squares with a pizza wheel and serve.

 TIP   *Feel free to buy prepared raw dough from your local pizza place if you don't have time to make your own.*

DRINKS

HIBISCUS ICED TEA

A jewel-toned iced tea is like a gift on the table. In addition to being beautiful, hibiscus tea is caffeine-free, so you can drink it whenever you want. If you can't find hibiscus tea bags, look for loose hibiscus leaves in the bulk food section of larger markets. *Serves 8*

8 hibiscus tea bags, or 1 ounce loose hibiscus leaves in a sachet for steeping loose tea leaves

¼ cup honey, plus more to taste

4 cups boiling water

¼ cup fresh mint leaves

Ice cubes

Dried hibiscus flowers, for garnish

HELPFUL TOOLS
Heatproof pitcher

1   In a large heatproof pitcher, combine the hibiscus tea bags or sachet, honey, and boiling water. Let steep for 1 hour at room temperature.

2   Remove the tea bags and refrigerate the tea for 1 hour, or until chilled.

3   Stir in the mint. Pour the hibiscus tea into ice-filled glasses, garnish with dried hibiscus flowers, and serve.

Cucumber Cooler
PAGE 151

Grapefruit Raspberry Sparkler
PAGE 152

Rosemary Blush
PAGE 154

CUCUMBER COOLER

Although nice in the evening, you can try this cucumber, lime, and mint combination paired with a daytime meal, too. When making, roll the whole lime a bit between the palm of your hand and the counter to loosen the inside, which makes it easier to juice. *Serves 4*

16 thin slices cucumber

10 fresh mint leaves

½ cup Simple Syrup (page 155)

½ cup fresh lime juice (from 4 large limes)

Ice cubes

4 cups club soda

Cucumber slices or ribbons, for garnish

HELPFUL TOOLS

Cocktail shaker

Muddler or wooden spoon

Coupe glasses or other fun shallow glasses

1   Combine the cucumber slices, mint leaves, and simple syrup in a shaker. Using a muddler or wooden spoon, muddle the ingredients together until very fragrant, about 1 minute.

2   Add the lime juice and 4 to 6 ice cubes, depending on the size. Place lid on the shaker to seal and shake vigorously for about 1 minute.

3   Open shaker and evenly divide the cucumber mixture among four shallow glasses. Add additional ice to each if needed. Top off each drink with an even portion of club soda, garnish with a cucumber wheel or ribbon, and serve.

If you have access to crushed ice, you could substitute it for the cubes in Step 3.

GRAPEFRUIT RASPBERRY SPARKLER

We learned a lot about making drinks (like muddling and balancing acid and sweet) by watching the bartenders at our parents' restaurants and came up with this drink by riffing on one of the most popular mocktails on one of the menus. (Don't be shy in the kitchen about learning a recipe and then adding your own twist!) Keep in mind that most drink concoctions and recipes are way too sweet. They might be good for the first taste, but remember, you want someone to drink a whole glass, not just one sip, so always sweeten drinks just a tad less than you think you should. *Serves 4*

1½ cups freshly squeezed pink grapefruit juice (from about 2 large pink grapefruit)

½ cup fresh raspberries, plus more for garnish

¼ cup Simple Syrup (page 155)

Ice cubes

4 cups sparkling water

Grapefruit wedges, for garnish

HELPFUL TOOLS

Large glass jar with lid

Wooden spoon or muddler

1 In a large glass jar with a lid, combine half the grapefruit juice, the raspberries, and the simple syrup. With a wooden spoon or muddler, crush the berries together to muddle. Add the remaining grapefruit juice, top the jar with the lid, then swirl to mix everything.

2 Evenly divide the juice mixture among four glasses filled with ice. Top off each glass with sparkling water. Garnish with additional raspberries and grapefruit wedges and serve.

TIP *Try adding mint to your liking during the muddling process for an added kick.*

Recipe pictured on page 150

ROSEMARY BLUSH

It might sound weird to use herbs in cold drinks, but they can give a drink a unique sense of balance that is usually hard to find in mocktails. The method of infusing rosemary into the simple syrup is a great way to bring forward the herb notes without overpowering the rest of the ingredients. *Serves 4*

1 cup Simple Syrup (page 155)

2 sprigs fresh rosemary, plus more for garnish

10 fresh strawberries, stem removed and cut into quarters

½ cup fresh lemon juice (from 3 lemons)

Ice cubes

1 cup sparkling water

HELPFUL TOOLS

Large glass with wide mouth

Muddler or wooden spoon

Rocks glasses

1   In a small saucepan, combine the simple syrup and rosemary and bring to a simmer over medium heat. Remove from the heat and discard the rosemary sprigs. Let cool slightly, then transfer to a wide-mouthed glass. Cover and chill the rosemary simple syrup in the refrigerator for 30 minutes.

2   Add the strawberries and lemon juice to the rosemary syrup. With a muddler or wooden spoon, crush and smash down the berries.

3   Spoon even amounts of the mixture into the bottom of four rocks glasses. Add a few ice cubes, then top off with sparkling water. Garnish with rosemary sprigs before serving.

 If you have an ice mold that makes large or extra-large cubes, use it to make ice for this drink.

Recipe pictured on page 150

SIMPLE SYRUP

It's a smart idea to have simple syrup on hand at all times, as it is a key ingredient in many drinks. It's beloved for iced beverages especially, because regular granulated sugar does not dissolve well in cold liquids. To infuse your simple syrup with a subtle flavor, add desired amount of a single flavoring, such as dried lavender, cardamom, rosemary, or chamomile, to the saucepan when making. Lavender syrup is also a lovely choice for drizzling on a fresh fruit salad! *Makes 1 quart*

2 cups water

2 cups granulated sugar

Optional: Approximately ¼ cup, or more to liking, of desired item to steep

HELPFUL TOOLS

Strainer or tea sachets for steeping, optional

1 Bring water to a boil in a medium saucepan. Once boiling, whisk in sugar and let dissolve completely. (If infusing an ingredient, add it to the pan with the cold water before it boils.)

2 Remove from the heat and let cool completely. Remove infused ingredients by straining or taking out sachets. Store syrup in an airtight container in the refrigerator for several months.

STRAWBERRY BANANA SMOOTHIE PLUS

The combo of strawberries and bananas is the gold standard of smoothies, and we've added a little something special by subbing almond milk for regular milk. To go fully dairy-free, use a coconut-based yogurt. *Serves 2 to 4, depending on glass size*

1 cup almond milk

¼ cup whole-milk yogurt or coconut-based yogurt

1 cup ice

2 cups frozen strawberries

1 banana, peeled and broken in chunks

1½ tablespoons honey

Fresh strawberries, for garnish, optional

HELPFUL TOOLS

Blender

Drinking straws

1 Place the almond milk and yogurt in a blender, followed by the ice, strawberries, banana, and honey. Blend on high speed until very smooth.

2 Pour into two to four glasses and garnish each with a fresh strawberry (if you like) and a straw.

If there's any leftover smoothie in the blender, use to fill ice pop molds and freeze to have pops on hand for snacks at another time.

DREAMY COOKIES & CREAM MILKSHAKE

The captivating spirit of a milkshake can grab you the moment you hear the whir of the blender, and can prove equally thrilling as you drink it! Every time we get our hands on one, we're as happy as can be. *Serves 2 to 4, depending on glass size*

6 cream-filled chocolate wafer cookies (Oreos), plus more for garnish

2½ cups vanilla ice cream, softened

¼ cup whole milk

2 teaspoons vanilla extract

Fresh cream, whipped to firm peaks (see page 126)

HELPFUL TOOLS

Blender

Wide straws

1   Place two to four tall glasses in the freezer to chill for 30 minutes.

2   In a blender, crush the cookies with a few good pulses. Add the ice cream, milk, and vanilla and blend until smooth.

3   Pour into the frozen glasses and garnish each with whipped cream and a whole cookie. Insert a straw, serve, and share—maybe.

Dreamy Cookies &
Cream Milkshake
PAGE 159

BEETROOT LATTE

This fun take on a traditional latte has popped up on coffee bar menus all over NYC. We love it because of the gorgeous color that comes from the beets, the natural sweetness, and the rich, smooth taste. It is a wonderful change from the usual hot drinks that we would normally make!

Serves 4

4 teaspoons beetroot powder, or 2 cups beet juice reduced to 2 tablespoons and cooled

½ teaspoon ground cinnamon, plus more for garnish

¼ teaspoon ground ginger

⅛ teaspoon freshly ground black pepper

5 cups almond milk

¼ cup honey

HELPFUL TOOLS

Milk frother, optional

1   In a medium saucepan, off heat, whisk together the beetroot powder, cinnamon, ginger, and pepper. Gradually whisk in 4 cups of the milk, then the honey.

2   Place the pan over medium-high heat and bring to a simmer, whisking constantly. Remove from the heat and ladle into mugs.

3   With a milk frother, steam the remaining 1 cup milk and spoon on top of each serving. (If a frother is not available, you can heat the milk and whisk by hand. It won't have the same tall, foamy result but will be equally as delicious.) Garnish with a dash of cinnamon on each.

TIPS

Soy or oat milk can be substituted for the almond milk. As with all dairy alternatives, look for one without a lot of added sugar or flavoring.

To prepare one single serving, you can make a batch of the spiced powder in Step 1 and then add about a teaspoon of the powder per one beverage. When ready, proceed with recipe for desired portion of milk and then froth milk as desired for the top.

PREMIER HOT CHOCOLATE

Here it is, the pro way to prepare hot chocolate! You'll need spices, two types of dairy—whole milk and heavy cream—and, of course, the highest-quality bittersweet chocolate you can get your hands on. Don't wait until the holidays for this amazing drink. Have it all year round. *Serves 4*

¼ cup heavy cream

½ cup chopped bittersweet chocolate

½ cup granulated sugar

2 cups whole milk

2 teaspoons vanilla extract

1 teaspoon ground cinnamon

¼ teaspoon freshly grated nutmeg

¼ teaspoon ground cloves

Freshly whipped cream (page 126), for garnish

HELPFUL TOOLS

Piping bag

Ladle

1 In a medium saucepan, heat the cream, chocolate, and sugar over low heat, whisking constantly, until the chocolate is melted and combined with the cream.

2 Gradually whisk in the milk, followed by vanilla, cinnamon, nutmeg, and cloves. Turn the heat to medium and continue to whisk until the mixture is hot but not boiling.

3 Fill a piping bag with the whipped cream, then snip off the end. With a ladle, divide the hot chocolate among four mugs, then pipe on whipped cream as tall as your heart desires.

NOTE OF THANKS

Guess what? Too many cooks in the kitchen might not be ideal for dinner, but it makes for a wonderful cookbook! Writing a book like this takes a lot of work and requires a large team to bring it to a reality. We're so incredibly lucky to have all these people supporting us.

MOM AND DAD, we thank you for encouraging our love of eating since the day we were born. Please keep teaching us, and we promise to keep cooking for you.

OUR GRANDPARENTS, MARIE AND FRAN, thank you for helping on this project, and more importantly, thank you for hosting as many family meals and memories as you possibly could! For as long as we can remember, you've played such a huge role in fostering our passion for food. Your love knows no end, and we are forever grateful to have you as our grandparents.

JAMES PATTERSON, a green light from you most certainly meant *Go, go, go!* We are humbled that you believed in us, in this project, and that there are many cooks out there who need a book like this for their home kitchens. We have been so honored to work with you and your **TEAM AT JIMMY PATTERSON BOOKS:** Ned Rust, Tracy Shaw, Laura Schreiber, Caitlyn Averett, Daniel Denning, Diana McElfresh, Erinn McGrath, Charlotte Lamontagne, Josh Johns, Elizabeth Blue Guess, Florence Yue, Ben Allen, Alexis Lassiter, Jordan Mondell, and Virginia Lawther. Thank you for fostering every single detail with incredible professionalism from idea to printed page. The gratitude we feel is tremendous. You all rock!

LUCI LEVERE, you took our concepts and recipes and made sure they were doable, legible, and delicious. We are so fortunate to have you as our counterpart in the kitchen. Your technique for cooking and your eye for styling continually impress. And thanks for your sunny smile on set — you brightened each and every moment!

GALE AND KC KRATT: wow! A grand *merci* for welcoming us all into your studio as if it were your home, listening to our ideas with careful consideration, and teaching us about professional photography with passion and excitement. Your images have made our food come to life and will help teach young cooks everywhere.

AMY DOYLE, we absolutely adore you! As usual, your candid photographs captured our spirit and our love for each other. Thank you for jumping in full force with us. We are lucky to know you and have you as part of our team.

ANTHONY CANDELLA, a salute to our fearless organizer. You kept this entire project on track. All areas felt your daily care — culinary, photography, styling, writing, taste testing…the list goes on and on. We will never forget your enthusiasm for making this project perfect, and the funny dance you were willing to do so George would happily cooperate.

LAURA PALESE, your creativity and eye for style has brought such a special element to this book. How did we get so lucky to have you on this project?! We love your work and can't wait for our next project (and dinner!) together again.

EVAN SUNG, after all was said and done with recipe testing, interior photos, and writing, we won the lottery by having you shoot the cover. You brought such calm and expertise to that day. Truly, it was an honor to have you take our picture, and it was a pleasure to laugh together.

ANDY McNICOL, cool girl, thanks for helping us navigate the waters on our first book. Hopefully this is the first of many! We will always sign on the line for you.

To all **THOSE WHO CONTRIBUTED THEIR HEARTS AND IN SOME CASES, THEIR SPECIAL PLACES, TO THIS BOOK ALONG THE WAY:** Eric Haugen, Molly Swanson, Lois Cahill, Jaret Keller, Tara Halper, Jill Gedra, Edward Forester, Jenny Link Kieffer, Steve Gabris, Maryellen Howe, Taymour Hallal, Chris Lospalluto, Will Pierce, Mariana Velazquez, Sarah Jane Cave, Andrew Trautman and Justin Smith of Remedy House, Tom Towers of Tom Towers Farm Market, Tim Finkle of RCR Yachts, the Niagara Falls Country Club, the Youngstown Yacht Club, and Rype Studios.

INDEX

A

almond butter
  banana muffins with, 4
  banana Nutella sandwiches
    with, 14–15
  snack balls with, 133
almond milk
  latte with, 162
  overnight oats with, 26
  smoothie with, 156–57
  substitutions for, 162
almonds
  banana muffins with, 3–4
  granola bars with, 130–31
  rice pilaf with, 101
  whipped cream with extract
    of, 126
apples
  crumble with, 116–17
  mustard potatoes with, 99–100
  soup with, 50
arugula
  egg and olive tartines with, 5–6
  salad with tomato and, 84–85
avocado
  chili with, 56–57
  chocolate mousse with, 122
  fish tacos with, 76, 78
  Greek Sunday morning with,
    10–11
  salad with grapefruit and, 31, 33
  toast topped with, 6–7

B

bacon
  chili with pancetta, 57
  turkey club sandwich with, 45
balls, power-up snack, 132–33, 139

bananas
  chocolate mousse with, 122
  flourless muffins with, 3–4
  sandwiches with, 14–15
  smoothie with, 156–57
bars, olive oil granola, 130–31
beans, chili with, 56–57
beef
  bistro hanger steak, 86–87
  braised short ribs, 88–89
  burgers of, 90–91
  meatballs with, 64
beetroot powder
  latte with, 162
  purple mustard with, 142
blending hot liquids, 42
blueberry crumb muffins, 2
bread
  avocado toast, 6–7
  garlic, 63, 65
  tomato and herb flat-, 128,
    144–45
  See also pita bread; sandwiches;
    tartines; tortillas
bread crumbs, pork Milanese with
  panko, 85
broccoli, steamed ponzu, 102–3
burgers, best messy, 90–91

C

cabbage, fish tacos with, 76, 78
cacio e pepe (cheese and pepper),
  60, 62
capers, tuna salad tartines with,
  38
carrots
  chop chop salad with, 30, 32
  Grandma's chicken noodle soup
    with, 53

honey, 96, 98
  short ribs braised with, 88–89
cashew butter, overnight oats
  with, 26
cauliflower, Mediterranean, 95,
  97
celery
  chop chop salad with, 30, 32
  Grandma's chicken noodle soup
    with, 53
cheese
  burgers with cheddar, 90
  cacio e pepe with pecorino
    Romano, 60, 62
  cast iron grilled, 40–41
  chili with Mexican, 56–57
  chop chop salad with Parmesan,
    30, 32
  country style salad with feta,
    32, 34
  crackers with cheddar, 127,
    135–36
  garlic bread with Parmesan, 65
  meatballs with Parmesan, 64
  pork Milanese with Parmesan,
    85
  risotto with Parmesan, 61
  scrambled eggs with Mexican,
    12–13
cherries, granola bars with,
  130–31
chia seeds
  overnight oats with, 26–27
  snack balls with, 132–33
chicken
  Grandma's soup with, 53, 64
  honey mustard skewered,
    80–81
  roasted spatchcock, 82–83

chickpeas
  chop chop salad with, 30, 32
  hummus of, 134–35
chili, game day pork, 56–57
chips
  homemade potato, 137–39
  sea salt kale, 140–41
chocolate
  brownie tart with, 110–11
  magic mousse, 122–23
  premier hot, 164–65
  shortbread with, 124–25, 127
  snack balls with, 132–33
  whipped cream with, 126
cinnamon
  crullers with, 8–9
  hot chocolate with, 165
  latte with, 162
clams, linguini with, 63, 67
club soda, cucumber cooler with, 151
cocoa powder. *See* chocolate
coconut milk
  popcorn soup with, 54
  rice cooked in, 68–69
coffee, brownie tart with, 110
cookies
  milkshake with, 158–61
  olive oil granola bar, 130–31
  vanilla bean shortbread, 124–25, 127
cooking tools and tips, xiv–xvi
corn, soups with, 48–49, 54–55
crab meat, chilled corn soup with, 48–49
crackers, everything cheddar, 127, 135–36
cranberries
  granola bars with, 130–31
  snack balls with, 132–33
cream
  hot chocolate with, 165
  milkshake with, 159

panna cotta with, 118
  whipped, 126
  See also ice cream
crudités, hummus with, 134–35
crullers, cinnamon sugar, 8–9
crumble, apple, 116–17
cucumbers
  cooler with, 150–51
  country style salad with, 33, 34

D

doughnuts, cinnamon sugar cruller, 8–9
dressings
  chop chop salad, 30
  shallot vinaigrette, 36–37
  tip for making, 37

E

eggplant, ratatouille with, 104–5
eggs
  avocado toast with, 6–7
  breakfast fried rice with, 19
  brownie tart with, 110
  meatballs with, 64
  Mexican scrambled, 12–13
  Middle Eastern, 16–17
  tartines with hardboiled, 5–6
egg whites
  French strawberry soufflés with, 113
  meringue clouds with, 120–21
  whipping, 114
English muffins, egg and olive tartines with, 5–6

F

fennel
  branzino with braised, 74–75
  tuna salad tartines with, 38–39
fish
  crispy skin salmon, 72–73
  steamed halibut, 68–69

tacos with, 76, 78–79
  tuna salad tartines, 38–39
  whole branzino, 74–75
flax seeds, snack balls with, 132–33
focaccia, tomato and herb, 128, 144–45

G

garlic
  bread toasted with, 63, 65
  linguini and clams with, 67
  short ribs braised with, 89
  spaghetti Bolognese with, 66
  spatchcock chicken with, 82–83
  spinach sautéed with, 94, 97
gelatin, panna cotta with, 118
granola
  Greek Sunday morning with, 11
  snack bars with, 130–31
grapefruit
  Greek Sunday morning with, 10–11
  salad with avocado and, 31, 33
  segmenting, 11
  sparkler with, 150, 152
Greek Sunday morning, 10–11

H

ham
  avocado toast with prosciutto, 6–7
  Parisian sandwich with, 46–47
hazelnuts
  banana Nutella sandwiches with, 14–15
  brownie tart with, 110–11
herbs
  butter with, 72–73
  mustard potatoes with, 99–100
  See also specific herb
hibiscus iced tea, 148–49

honey
    carrots glazed with, 96, 98
    chicken skewers with, 80–81
    Greek Sunday morning with, 11
    hibiscus iced tea with, 148
    latte with, 162
    smoothie with, 156
    snack balls with, 133
hummus, creamy, 134–35

I

ice cream
    brownie tart with, 110
    cookies and cream milkshake
      with, 159

K

kale chips, sea salt, 140–41
kitchen tools, xiv–xv

L

lamb, Middle Eastern eggs with,
    16–17
latte, beetroot, 162–63
leeks
    popcorn soup with, 54
    short ribs braised with, 89
lemon
    apple crumble with, 117
    blueberry crumb muffins with,
      2
    branzino with, 74–75
    country style salad with, 33,
      34
    halibut steamed with, 68–69
    hummus with, 134–35
    mustard potatoes with, 99
    raspberry sauce with, 25
    rosemary blush with, 154
    shrimp scampi with, 70–71
    tuna salad tartines with, 38
lettuce, Bibb
    burgers with, 90–91

with shallot vinaigrette, 36–37
    turkey club sandwich with,
      44–45
    See also arugula; romaine hearts
lime
    broccoli steamed with, 102
    chili with, 56–57
    cucumber cooler with, 151
    fish tacos with, 76, 78
    popcorn soup with, 54
    tropical pineapple and, 108–9

M

maple syrup
    granola bars with, 130
    overnight oats with, 26
    pancakes topped with, 22–24
mayonnaise
    burger sauce with, 90
    grilled cheese with, 41
    turkey club with, 44–45
meatballs, classic, 62, 64
meringue, pastel clouds of, 120–21
milk
    cookies and cream milkshake
      with, 158–61
    hot chocolate with, 164–65
    See also almond milk; coconut
      milk
mint
    cucumber cooler with, 150–51
    grapefruit raspberry sparkler
      with, 152
    hibiscus iced tea with, 148–49
mousse, magic chocolate, 122–23
muffins
    blueberry crumb, 2–3
    flourless banana, 3–4
    tartines with English, 5–6
mustard
    chicken skewers with, 80–81
    potatoes with, 99–100
    pretzels with purple, 142–43

N

noodles
    braised short ribs with, 88–89
    Grandma's soup with, 53, 64
Nutella, sandwiches with banana
    and, 14–15
nuts. *See* almonds; hazelnuts; pine
    nuts; pistachios

O

oats
    granola bars with, 130–31
    on-the-go overnight, 26–27
    snack balls with, 132–33
    streusel topping with, 116–17
olives
    country style salad with, 32,
      34
    egg tartines with, 5–6
    tuna salad tartines with, 38
onions
    arugula tomato salad with,
      84–85
    chili with, 57
    Grandma's chicken noodle soup
      with, 53
    grapefruit avocado salad with,
      31, 33
    ratatouille with, 104–5
    short ribs braised with, 89
    See also leeks; shallots
orange
    broccoli steamed with, 102
    carrots glazed with, 98
    Greek Sunday morning with,
      10–11

P

pancakes
    lemon raspberry, 22, 24
    perfect, 22–23
pancetta, chili with, 57
panna cotta, summer, 118

parsley
> branzino with, 74–75
> garlic bread with, 65
> Grandma's chicken noodle soup with, 53
> linguini with, 67
> meatballs with, 64
> Middle Eastern eggs with, 16–17

pasta
> cacio e pepe, 60, 62
> linguini with clams, 63, 67
> shrimp scampi with, 71
> spaghetti Bolognese, 62, 66

peaches, panna cotta with, 118

peanut butter, granola bars with, 130

pepper, cacio e pepe with black, 60, 62

peppers, red bell
> chop chop salad with, 30, 32
> ratatouille with, 104–5
> roasting, 38
> tuna salad tartines with, 38

pineapple
> choosing ripe, 109
> tropical, 108–9

pine nuts
> Middle Eastern eggs with, 16–17
> squash and apple soup with, 50
> toasting, 50

pistachios, shortbread with, 124–25, 127

pita bread
> country style salad with, 34
> Middle Eastern eggs with, 16–17

ponzu, broccoli steamed with, 102–3

popcorn, soup with, 54–55

poppy seeds, cheddar crackers with, 127, 135–36

porcini powder, 66

pork
> chili with, 56–57
> crispy Milanese, 84–85
> meatballs with, 64
> pounding bone-in, 85
> *See also* bacon; ham; sausage

potatoes
> homemade chips, 137–39
> mustard, 99–100

pretzels, soft baked, 139, 142–43

prosciutto, avocado toast with, 6–7

pumpkin, popcorn soup with, 54

pumpkin seeds, granola bars with, 130–31

R

radishes, chili with, 56–57

raisins
> rice pilaf with, 100–101
> snack balls with, 132–33

raspberries
> Greek Sunday morning with, 10–11
> sauce of fresh, 22, 24, 25
> sparkler with, 150, 152

ratatouille, xi, 104–5

rice
> breakfast fried, 18–20
> fragrant pilaf, 100–101
> halibut with coconut, 68–69
> risotto with, 61, 63

risotto 3X, 61, 63

romaine hearts
> chop chop salad with, 30, 32
> country style salad with, 32–33, 34

rosemary
> blush with, 150, 154
> focaccia with, 128, 144–45
> potato chips with, 137

S

salads
> arugula tomato, 84–85
> chop chop, 30, 32
> country style, 32–34
> grapefruit avocado, 31, 33
> tartines with tuna, 38–39

sandwiches
> banana Nutella, 14–15
> best messy burger, 90–91
> cast iron grilled cheese, 40–41
> Parisian ham, 46–47
> short stack turkey club, 44–45
> *See also* tartines

sauces
> burger, 90–91
> fresh raspberry, 22, 24, 25
> purple mustard, 142–43
> *See also* soy sauce

sausage, spaghetti Bolognese with, 66

scallions, chili with, 57

sesame seeds
> breakfast fried rice with, 18–20
> cheddar crackers with, 127, 135–36
> Mediterranean cauliflower with, 95

shallots
> bistro hanger steak with, 86–87
> vinaigrette with, 36–37

shopping tips, xvi

shortbread, vanilla bean, 124–25, 127

shrimp scampi, 70–71

skewers, honey mustard chicken, 80–81

smoothie, strawberry banana, 156–57

soufflés, French strawberry, 113–15

soups
> butternut squash and apple, 50

chilled corn, 48–49

crazy popcorn, 54–55

Grandma's chicken noodle, 53, 64

meatball, 64

oven roasted tomato, 40, 42

soy sauce

breakfast fried rice with, 19

broccoli steamed with, 102

spaghetti

Bolognese, 62, 66

shrimp scampi with, 71

spinach, sautéed, 94, 97

squash

ratatouille with, 104–5

soup with butternut, 50

strawberries

French soufflés with, 113–15

rosemary blush with, 150, 154

smoothie with, 156–57

streusel topping, 116–17

sugar

simple syrup of, 155

vanilla, 125

sunflower seeds, granola bars with, 130–31

syrup, simple, 155

drinks with, 151, 152, 154

See also maple syrup

T

tacos, build-your-own fish, 76, 78–79

tapenade for egg and olive tartines, 5–6

tart, decadent brownie, 110–11

tartines

egg and olive, 5–6

tuna salad, 38–39

tea, hibiscus iced, 148–49

tomatoes

burgers with, 90

chili with, 56–57

country style salad with, 33, 34

focaccia with, 128, 144–45

meatball soup with, 64

salad with arugula and, 84–85

soup of oven roasted, 40, 42

spaghetti Bolognese with, 66

turkey club sandwich with, 45

tortillas

for fish tacos, 76, 78–79

Mexican scrambled eggs with, 12–13

turkey club, short stack, 44–45

V

vanilla

shortbread cookies with, 124–25, 127

sugar infused with, 125

whipped cream with, 126

veal, meatballs with, 64

vinaigrette, shallot, 36–37

W

watercress, grapefruit avocado salad with, 31, 33

wine

short ribs braised with, 89

spaghetti Bolognese with, 66

Y

yogurt

chicken skewers with, 81

Greek Sunday morning with, 10–11

panna cotta with, 118

smoothie with, 156

Z

zucchini, ratatouille with, 104–5

ABOUT THE AUTHORS

Madeline and Anna Zakarian are the daughters of Iron Chef Geoffrey Zakarian. In addition to attending school, they play multiple sports, instruments, and tricks on each other. When they are not cooking at home or on TV, they share their love of food by volunteering with their parents and brother for City Harvest.

Anna,
AS DESCRIBED BY
MADELINE IN TEN WORDS

Caring, Sweet, Loud,
Smart, Crazy, Loving, Enthusiastic,
Musical, Sporty, Artistic

Madeline,
AS DESCRIBED BY
ANNA IN TEN WORDS

Stylish, Smart, Mature,
Funny, Musical, Artistic, Dramatic,
Organized, Loving, Amazing